# TRUTH
## WITHOUT APOLOGY

# TRUTH
## WITHOUT APOLOGY

### FOR THOSE TIRED OF SWEET LIES

## ACHARYA PRASHANT

HarperCollins *Publishers* India

First published in India by HarperCollins *Publishers* 2025
HarperCollins *Publishers* India, Cyber City,
Building 10-A, Gurugram, Haryana – 122002, India
www.harpercollins.co.in

4 6 8 10 9 7 5

Copyright © Acharya Prashant 2025

P-ISBN: 978-93-6989-657-8
E-ISBN: 978-93-6989-032-3

The views and opinions expressed in this book are the author's own and the facts are as reported by him, and the publishers are not in any way liable for the same.

Acharya Prashant asserts the moral right
to be identified as the author of this work.

All rights reserved. No part of this publication may be reproduced, stored in a retrieval system, or transmitted, in any form or by any means, electronic, mechanical, photocopying, recording or otherwise, without the prior permission of the publishers.

Without limiting the exclusive rights of any author, contributor or the publisher of this publication, any unauthorized use of this publication to train generative artificial intelligence (AI) technologies is expressly prohibited. HarperCollins also exercise their rights under Article 4(3) of the Digital Single Market Directive 2019/790 and expressly reserve this publication from the text and data-mining exception.

Typeset in 11/14 Merriweather 96pt
by HarperCollins *Publishers* India Pvt. Ltd

Printed and bound at
Gopsons Papers Pvt. Ltd., Noida

This book is produced from independently certified FSC® paper to ensure responsible forest management.

HarperCollins Publishers, Macken House, 39/40 Mayor Street Upper,
Dublin 1, D01 C9W8, Ireland

# Contents

Introduction — xiii

## THE LIE CALLED YOU

01  You Exist in Their Eyes? — 3
02  Why Do People Show Off? — 5
03  To Know Yourself, Watch Yourself — 7
04  Self-Love Isn't Self-Lies — 9
05  Your Life Is the Mirror — 11
06  Sleepwalking through Life — 13
07  Catching Yourself Red-Handed — 15
08  Stealing from Your Own Pocket — 17
09  The Most Dangerous Wound Is Self-Inflicted — 18
10  The Victim Card — 19
11  Stop Pampering the Wound — 20
12  No Belief Is Sacred — 21
13  Grow, Don't Just Glow — 23
14  Stop Defending Your Weaknesses — 24
15  Improvement Is Not a Strategy — 25
16  Let the Petty Go — 26
17  Behind Your Back, Something Is Ticking — 27

## Contents

### FEAR: THE INNER DICTATOR

| | | |
|---|---|---|
| 18 | When the Mind Growls, Listen | 31 |
| 19 | Fear Is a Liar, Test It | 33 |
| 20 | Fear Isn't Weakness, It's a Message | 35 |
| 21 | With Trembling Hands | 37 |
| 22 | The Courage to Walk Away | 39 |
| 23 | Confidence Is Fear | 40 |
| 24 | Fear Never Comes as Fear | 42 |
| 25 | The Next Step Is Enough | 44 |

### THE HUNGER THAT CONSUMES

| | | |
|---|---|---|
| 26 | The Punishment Called Entertainment | 49 |
| 27 | Eh! Go, Get a Life | 51 |
| 28 | You Invited the Thief | 53 |
| 29 | Distractions Don't Win, Weak Goals Lose | 55 |
| 30 | No Trophies, Just Play | 57 |
| 31 | Before You Win, Ask: What Are You Winning | 59 |
| 32 | The Myth of Free Time | 60 |
| 33 | Nothing Lasts but the Joke | 62 |
| 34 | Joy: The Hardest Pleasure | 64 |
| 35 | Your Goals Are Not Yours | 66 |
| 36 | Sex Isn't the Problem, Emptiness Is | 68 |
| 37 | The Final Cure for Addiction | 70 |
| 38 | Keep the Man Aside | 72 |
| 39 | Beyond Happiness | 74 |
| 40 | The Earth Burns because You Do | 76 |
| 41 | Don't Kill Desire. Purify It. | 79 |

## Contents

### WORK, WILL, AND THE RIGHT FIGHT

| | | |
|---|---|---|
| 42 | Continuity, Not Perfection | 83 |
| 43 | From One Fire to the Next | 85 |
| 44 | Beat Yourself | 87 |
| 45 | Deadlines to Discipline to Freedom | 89 |
| 46 | Win Small, Win Often | 91 |
| 47 | The Joy of Right Action | 92 |
| 48 | Fill Your Life, or It Will Fill Itself | 94 |
| 49 | Impossible Is the Invitation | 96 |
| 50 | Loveless Work Is Joyless Life | 98 |
| 51 | The Battle Worth Fighting | 100 |
| 52 | A Work Worth Your Life | 102 |
| 53 | Immersed or Lost? | 104 |
| 54 | Not Passion. Not Pressure. Just Love. | 106 |
| 55 | Entrepreneurship as a Sacred Calling | 108 |
| 56 | Sacred Selfishness | 110 |
| 57 | A Huge Kitchen Called Life | 112 |
| 58 | The Jungle in a Necktie | 114 |
| 59 | The Burden of False Duties | 116 |

### RELATIONSHIPS: THE GREAT ILLUSION

| | | |
|---|---|---|
| 60 | Loneliness Is the First Teacher | 121 |
| 61 | Loneliness Is the Crowd Within | 123 |
| 62 | Purpose First, Person Later | 125 |
| 63 | Valuable or Merely Vulnerable? | 126 |
| 64 | Hurt Is When Fantasy Breaks | 127 |
| 65 | Desire Invests, Love Nurtures | 128 |

## Contents

| | | |
|---|---|---|
| 66 | Half and Half Is a Quarter | 129 |
| 67 | When Closeness Becomes a Cage | 131 |
| 68 | Love That Sets You Free | 132 |
| 69 | Mr Hormones Again! | 134 |
| 70 | I Love You, Seriously? | 136 |
| 71 | Love That Breaks under Heat | 137 |
| 72 | Love beyond Fantasy | 139 |
| 73 | Echoes of Emptiness | 140 |
| 74 | Love You as You Are? | 142 |
| 75 | Romancing Infinity | 143 |
| 76 | Tried Attachment? Now Try Love | 145 |
| 77 | You Become What You Love | 147 |
| 78 | Love Happens Outside the Script | 148 |
| 79 | Their Longing Is Yours | 149 |
| 80 | Be Whole before You Belong | 151 |
| 81 | Real Love Is Never Incidental | 152 |
| 82 | Watch the Effect, Not the Person | 154 |
| 83 | Blind Union, Lifelong Prison | 155 |
| 84 | Loving the Person or the Ghost? | 157 |
| 85 | Beyond Forgiveness | 159 |

### THOUGHT, BELIEF, AND THE TRAP OF KNOWLEDGE

| | | |
|---|---|---|
| 86 | The Stainless Mind | 163 |
| 87 | Fluency without Insight Is Noise | 165 |
| 88 | You Can't Create Creativity | 167 |
| 89 | No Habit Is a Good Habit | 169 |
| 90 | Stay Uncertain, Stay Alive | 171 |

## Contents

| | | |
|---|---|---|
| 91 | The Blabber We Call Life | 173 |
| 92 | Why Motivation Fails | 175 |
| 93 | Why Self-Help Doesn't Help | 177 |
| 94 | Freedom from Positivity | 179 |
| 95 | Courage without Clarity Is Hysteria | 181 |
| 96 | Clarity Leaves No Alternatives | 182 |
| 97 | Beyond Borrowed Light | 184 |
| 98 | Most 'Scriptures' Are Just Old Books | 186 |
| 99 | If Truth Hurts, Niceness Kills | 188 |
| 100 | Outer Knowledge, Inner Darkness | 190 |
| 101 | Slaves of Approval, Strangers to Truth | 192 |
| 102 | Missing the Obvious | 194 |
| 103 | Laughing at Your Own Idiocy | 196 |
| 104 | The Power of Collective Stupidity | 198 |
| 105 | Wake Up before You Die | 200 |

### SOCIETY AND THE GAME OF OTHERS

| | | |
|---|---|---|
| 106 | Gossip Bonds the Insecure | 203 |
| 107 | Live Healthy in a Sick World | 205 |
| 108 | Give Yourself a Second Birth | 207 |
| 109 | When Success Fails the Self | 209 |
| 110 | Not Every Crime Screams | 211 |
| 111 | They Sell You the Wound, Then the Cure | 213 |
| 112 | Sacred Dissatisfaction | 215 |
| 113 | Born Animal, Meant to Rise | 217 |
| 114 | Not Toward Each Other, but Upward | 218 |
| 115 | Do They Love You—or Limit You? | 219 |

| | | |
|---|---|---|
| 116 | Jealousy: The Pain of Borrowed Identity | 220 |
| 117 | Technology Isn't the Problem, You Are | 222 |
| 118 | Good Spirituality Is Good Economics | 224 |
| 119 | Love Reflects the Self | 226 |
| 120 | Where Rape Really Begins | 228 |
| 121 | The Third Woman | 230 |
| 122 | The Industry of Incompleteness | 232 |
| 123 | The Emotional Engine of Climate Collapse | 234 |
| 124 | Parent, First Raise Yourself | 236 |
| 125 | The Holy Eight-Step Suicide | 238 |

## SUFFERING: THE GATE TO SINCERITY

| | | |
|---|---|---|
| 126 | Even Wounds Can Smile | 243 |
| 127 | Stop Collecting Wounds | 244 |
| 128 | All Is Well, until It Isn't | 246 |
| 129 | The Past Is the Present | 248 |
| 130 | Stop Choosing Misery | 250 |
| 131 | The Plumcake or the Truth? | 251 |
| 132 | Say Hello to Pain | 253 |
| 133 | Pain in Installments | 255 |
| 134 | You Repeat the Same Mistake a Hundred Times | 257 |
| 135 | You Consent to Your Suffering | 259 |
| 136 | Outgrow the One Who Erred | 261 |
| 137 | The Fire Inside, the Ashes Outside | 263 |
| 138 | Better Bleed for Truth Than Shine for Lies | 265 |

Contents

## THE CALL TO INNER FREEDOM

| | | |
|---|---|---|
| 139 | Too Smart to Be Wise | 269 |
| 140 | If Everything Goes, What Remains? | 271 |
| 141 | Am I Fulfilled? Who Cares! | 273 |
| 142 | Has Life Even Begun? | 275 |
| 143 | Better a Bloody Nose Than a Bleeding Heart | 277 |
| 144 | The Body Will Veto Liberation | 279 |
| 145 | Already Home | 281 |
| 146 | Play through Pain | 283 |
| 147 | Our Programmed Emotions | 285 |
| 148 | You Become What You Absorb | 287 |
| 149 | How Much Darkness Did You Leave Behind? | 288 |
| 150 | This Is Not Your Destiny! | 290 |
| 151 | Remember the Truth, Not the Noise | 292 |
| 152 | Stop Meditating, Go Watch TV | 293 |
| 153 | Dig the Dirt, Find the Diamond | 295 |
| 154 | Break Out of Your Shell | 296 |
| 155 | Ignore the Small | 297 |
| 156 | The Cage Was Never Outside | 298 |
| 157 | Time Doesn't Fly, You Drift | 299 |
| 158 | One Day Has Infinite Time | 300 |
| 159 | You're Not Lazy. You're Loveless. | 302 |
| 160 | Stop Waiting to Be Saved | 303 |
| 161 | You Are Not Born Alone | 304 |
| 162 | The Cage Feeds, the Sky Frees | 306 |

| | | |
|---|---|---|
| 163 | Give Wings, Not Chains | 308 |
| 164 | The Ancient Battle Within | 310 |
| 165 | Jump before You're Ready | 312 |

## TRUTH: THE ONLY AUTHORITY

| | | |
|---|---|---|
| 166 | The Past Stays Only If You Feed It | 317 |
| 167 | A Heap of Unkept Promises | 319 |
| 168 | The World Shakes Only the Shaken | 321 |
| 169 | No New Path, Just New Eyes | 322 |
| 170 | The End of Motivation, the Start of Clarity | 324 |
| 171 | Don't Fear the Cost of Freedom | 326 |
| 172 | Your First Love Must Be Your Highest Self | 327 |
| 173 | This Chemical Existence | 329 |
| 174 | Relaxed. And Dangerous. | 330 |
| 175 | Succeeding, or Being Owned? | 332 |
| 176 | Already Rich, Just Forgot | 334 |
| 177 | Find Your Flower | 336 |
| 178 | Why Remain Small? | 338 |
| 179 | Choose a Goal You Can Never Reach | 340 |
| 180 | Only Your Choice Matters | 342 |

# Introduction

This book is not here to entertain or soothe. It is meant for the reader who has begun to see the cost of self-deception.

*Truth without Apology* is not a gentle invitation, but a direct encounter. Every page confronts the reader with sharp clarity. Every line is meant to expose, not embellish. What you hold in your hands is not a polished theory or a self-help guide. It is a series of piercing illuminations.

Most human suffering is not due to lack of information or opportunity, but due to our stubborn loyalty to lies: the lies we inherit, the lies we tell ourselves, the lies we decorate in the name of culture, ambition, pleasure, relationships, even virtue. What happens when someone stops negotiating with these lies? What remains when all that is false is no longer allowed to hide behind social justification or emotional excuse?

This book is for those ready to confront these questions, and more. It doesn't offer a method. It does not ask for your belief. It simply lays bare the workings of the mind and the mechanisms of self-deception with a kind of precision we're often too scared to seek. The clarity it points to is not the product of imagination or tradition. It arises when one is willing to observe honestly, without filters, without defence, without escape.

The topics are wide-ranging: fear, ambition, love, loneliness, desire, self-worth. But the movement is singular—a movement toward clear seeing. Not thinking. Not hoping. Not reacting. Just seeing. And once we really see, change no longer feels like an effort. It becomes inevitable.

Some readers may find these insights unsettling. That's because the inner house we live in is constructed out of avoidance: avoidance of pain, avoidance of uncertainty, avoidance of inquiry. What this book offers is not comfort, but the courage to face discomfort for the sake of something real. It is a reminder that anything worth having must come at the cost of illusion.

But there is no cynicism here. No bitterness. The tone is neither harsh nor indulgent. There is love here, though not the kind the world is used to. This is a love that does not pamper or flatter, and has no interest in making you feel temporarily better. It is the kind of love that burns down what is false so that the truth may breathe. It may look like severity from the outside. But those who stay long enough will sense its tenderness.

There are no techniques to master, no path to chart out. The reader is simply being invited to pause and observe—to examine their decisions, their patterns, their hidden fears, their daily compulsions. And in that honest looking, to taste the possibility of living differently.

Peace does not come from hoping, wishing, or waiting. It comes from seeing things as they are, and dropping what doesn't serve that seeing.

This book is a mirror. Whether the reader chooses to look or turn away is entirely their freedom. But one should know: what is avoided today quietly becomes one's master tomorrow.

And if one dares to look honestly, even once, they may find that freedom was never as far as it seemed.

# THE LIE
# CALLED YOU

◆·◆·◆

# 01 | You Exist in Their Eyes?

> *"Reducing dependencies, finding your authentic self: that is the key to living fearlessly."*

When you blindly accept what the world says about you, you hand it power. You make the world your judge, and your master.

The way our species has evolved, the way we are born, we lack direct vision of ourselves. We cannot see ourselves inwardly. So we rely on others. We look at ourselves through their eyes. And the moment we do that, we become enslaved. Our very sense of existence now depends on them.

Terrible? Yes. But true.

Where there is dependence, there must be fear.

Is it still a mystery why we are afraid of others? It's not a personal shortcoming. It's the universal consequence of psychological dependence.

If you want to live without fear, you must investigate your dependencies. Ask: *Where have I outsourced my sense of worth?*

Cooperation is beautiful. Collaboration is necessary. But existential dependence is bondage. A business needing raw materials is natural. But the mind needing approval to feel worthy? That's sickness.

## You Exist in Their Eyes?

The body can be part of society. You can live among people, work with them, speak with them. But can you do all that while being inwardly free?

Why not?

Why must relatedness come at the cost of your sovereignty?

Why must love come bundled with fear?

It is possible to be among others, yet not belong to them. Possible to listen, yet not be swayed. Possible to seek feedback with humility, yet not be possessed by it. That is real fearlessness.

# 02 | Why Do People Show Off?

> *The exhibitionist mind seeks validation through others' approval, turning life into a constant display of possessions and relationships. The need to show off betrays a deeper insecurity: a life lived for external applause, never for inner strength or freedom.*

You go to a shop to buy clothes. What do you look for? Good to touch, good to wear, must look expensive, must not look cheap. That's how you pick a shirt. And when you choose a husband or a wife, it's the same checklist: *Good to look at, feels comfortable around me, and doesn't look cheap when we walk together.* It is the same mind at work.

Observe yourself in a garments shop, there you'll see the story of your life. If you are an exhibitionist choosing clothes—*A little lower neckline, a bit higher on the thigh*—you'll be the same with partners: *See my new puppy! I mean my new boyfriend. Or hey, don't you fancy my trophy wife?*

People display their cars. They display their houses. They display their lovers. They display their babies. It's all one continuous marketplace of validation.

## Why Do People Show Off?

What is the exhibitionist mind? It has lost the capacity to look directly at itself. It sees itself only through borrowed eyes. Its self-worth hangs on what others say. It lives a duplicate, second-hand life. If others praise it, it feels worthy. If others scorn it, it collapses. This is a terrible slavery: running breathless after the approval of strangers.

And the saddest part? This slavery is self-chosen and entirely unnecessary. One could instead choose strength. One could choose independence. Freedom is far more joyous than any borrowed applause.

# 03 | To Know Yourself, Watch Yourself

> *Who you really are is shown not by what you claim, but by what you pursue, what occupies your mind, and what you commit to."*

If you truly want to discover who you are, don't start by asking philosophical questions. Start with facts. Start with observation: not of the world, but of yourself.

See where your time goes.

See what repeatedly fills your thoughts.

See what kind of work earns you money.

See where that money is spent.

See what your heart secretly longs for.

See what you avoid. See what you are afraid to lose.

And you will begin to know who you are, not in theory, but in truth.

We all carry respectable self-images. *I am spiritual,* or *I care about justice,* or *I want to grow.* But look closely: most of these are aspirational claims, not honest confessions. The ego wants to appear evolved. But identity is not revealed by what you *say* you want. It is revealed by what you *actually* chase.

You are not your declared values. You are your lived patterns.

Where your feet walk, where your eyes linger, what keeps you restless at night: these are the true indicators. These are your teachers.

To know yourself, don't look at what you celebrate. Look at what you tolerate. Don't look at what you post. Look at what you protect. Don't look at your wishes. Look at your compulsions.

The honest self-observer begins to see: *I am not what I thought I was. I am deeply conditioned. My fears, cravings, and attachments run deeper than I admit.* This seeing is painful, but it is also the beginning of freedom.

Knowing yourself does not mean building a better image. It means watching the false one crumble.

So don't be in a rush to change yourself. First, be silent and watch. Let the truth emerge, raw, unfiltered. To know yourself is not to create a self. It is to become aware of how much of you is borrowed, automatic, and false.

To know yourself, watch yourself.

Honestly. Repeatedly. Relentlessly.

This alone is the beginning of a real spiritual life.

# 04 | Self-Love Isn't Self-Lies

> *Self-love is not about feeling good, but about being ruthlessly true to oneself. Self-awareness is self-love, self-indulgence is self-deception.*

Truth rarely feels good. It cuts. It exposes. It demolishes comfort.

Let the world chatter. People are entitled to their noisy opinions: on your accent, your skin, your clothes, your voice. These are externals. Let them say what they will.

But when it comes to your fundamental worth, your very being, absolutely no one has the right to pronounce judgment. Not even your closest ones. That is a sacred space. Guard it fiercely.

Only one entity can know you for what you really are, and that is you. But not as your own advocate. Be your own strictest examiner: honest, uncompromising. When you do that, the world's judgments, whether applause or ridicule, lose their grip on you.

Next time someone flatters you, do not swell. Next time someone criticizes you, do not shrink. Both are just flickers. At best, raw data. Not truths. Not verdicts. Just feedback which maybe useful, or usually irrelevant.

## Self-Love Isn't Self-Lies

Do not hang your sense of self on their shaky strings.

That is self-love. Not softness. Not sugar. But fierce awareness. Relentless honesty.

Ah, the fierce, liberating joys of self-awareness!

## 05 | Your Life Is the Mirror

> *Observe your own life, and you will know the Truth."*

We live in furious haste, utterly absorbed in distractions, rarely pausing to observe the one thing that truly matters: our own life. Isn't it essential to relieve the mind of its constant preoccupations? To give it space, silence, and sincerity, so it may finally see itself with clarity?

Ask yourself: What exactly are you doing, and why? Why this relentless noise, this gnawing restlessness, this dull boredom?

Why do you remain confused, insecure, constantly hungry for company? Why does even the whisper of solitude unsettle you? Why does the future evoke nothing but a see-saw of hope and fear?

Have you ever truly loved? Do you even begin to understand what it means to live?

These aren't abstract philosophical riddles. These are urgent, concrete questions bleeding through your everyday life. Unless you are deeply asleep or constantly fleeing from yourself, these questions will arise.

You've accepted a certain pattern as the norm. But why? Why not examine it with honesty and intelligence? Why not turn inward with the same sharpness you apply to the world?

This is your life: your one, fleeting, precious life. Observe it.

Not through society's lens. Not through the prism of borrowed values. Observe it with naked awareness. See what you chase, what you fear, what you compulsively repeat. No excuses. No drama. Just direct perception.

That is your deepest responsibility.

And when the mind begins to observe itself truthfully, something shifts. Not the cheap thrill you mistake for happiness, but the deep joy of clarity arises. Not excitement, but vitality. Not comfort, but liberation.

That clarity is your highest possibility. And nothing—not your past, not your suffering, not your beliefs—should be allowed to take it from you.

# 06 | Sleepwalking through Life

> "Man lives like a machine: programmed, predictable, and unconscious. What makes it worse is the illusion that we are choosing freely. See how deeply scripted your actions are, how borrowed your motivations. In that honest seeing, something real begins."

Remember class six? You were told, *Study hard, get good marks.*

Why? So your parents could boast to neighbours and relatives.

And when you didn't study, carrots were dangled: *Do well, and we'll buy you that toy.*

External motivation. External pressure. External rewards.

Then came class ten. The story shifted. *These marks will matter in job interviews.* So you bent your back, memorised more textbooks.

Then class twelve. *Critical year. Entrance exams. Your future depends on this.* So again, you slogged, exhausted and afraid.

And now? You want to extend the same stale story. Just add another dreary chapter to the same predictable script.

You have been a machine all your life, chasing numbers. Marks. Percentages. Ranks.

And you think it will stop? It never stops.

Soon it becomes salary, just another number.

Then come LinkedIn connections.

Then promotions and designations. Or an ambitious startup, so you can chase even bigger numbers.

Then you build a house, start a family, plan retirement.

All on pre-decided lines. All equally uninspired.

If this same story is being stretched like stale dough, tell me, what is the difference between that class six child and this seasoned professional?

Where is the growth?

Where is the movement?

Where is the learning?

Where is the evolution?

Are you really going ahead, or are you just running in circles, enacting the same script on different stages?

At one point you were a child. Then you became a teenager. Then a young man or woman. Then a professional. Then a husband or wife. Then a mother or father.

Different labels, different costumes, different stages, but the same old script running underneath. And none of it really written by you.

You are acting, but do you even know why there is action? You are moving, but do you know where you are going? You are alive, but are you awake?

Or are you just sleepwalking through life, repeating an old story that was never yours to begin with?

Do you really know who you are?

# 07 | Catching Yourself Red-Handed

> *There is great fun in catching your own inner mischief red-handed."*

Catch yourself when your mind is wandering into fantasy. Catch yourself when fear creeps in or insecurity whispers. The moment you spot a state of mind, it begins to lose its hold. All these hidden tendencies thrive only in darkness. They are like vampires. Shine the light of attention on them, and they shrivel away.

Your random thoughts, your jealousies, your anxieties: watch them. Just watch. The instant you see them clearly, their power starts dissolving. To catch something is to observe it. To observe is to expose it. And exposure is the beginning of freedom.

This is not an exotic technique. It is simple, so simple it feels almost disappointing to the restless mind. But it is rare, because we are determined to look everywhere except within. And what does it mean to look within? It means to look at one's impulses, feelings, thoughts, desires, and actions. There is no other 'within' to look at.

Look at how you live. You have no real understanding of why you do what you do. Today your mind drifts in one direction. Tomorrow, it lunges somewhere else. And you never pause to ask what is this movement, what is this restlessness.

External forces keep crashing over you in waves: temptations, fears, pressures. The mind gets tossed around, confused and exhausted. And still, you don't look within.

Remember, the functioning of the mind is understood by watching the mind. The laws of science do not come from imagination or belief, but from observation. The same applies here. Observe yourself like a scientist: honestly, patiently, without judgment.

To observe the ego is to begin dissolving the ego. And to dissolve the ego is to reclaim yourself. Only a free mind can make clear decisions about work, love, and family.

The quality of your mind is the quality of your life. The freedom of your mind is the only real freedom.

Catch yourself. Watch yourself. Observe yourself relentlessly.

That is the door to liberation.

# 08 | Stealing from Your Own Pocket

> *One lies to himself, and then believes his own lies. You may not deceive others for long, but you can deceive yourself all your life."*

Why do we call it theft only when you steal from someone else?

Is it not theft when you rob yourself of your own highest possibility? How is that any less criminal? Are we not guilty, first of all, toward ourselves?

If I snatch what is rightfully yours, you call it theft. If I plunder your house, you demand punishment. But what if I plunder my own house? What if I deny myself what I truly deserve to become? Is that not an even deeper theft?

Stealing from others is punished by society.

Stealing from yourself is punished by life itself.

Such is the law.

# 09 | The Most Dangerous Wound Is Self-Inflicted

> *A choice made in ignorance is not a choice. It's just an accident waiting to happen."*

Nobody knowingly chooses self-harm. Whatever we do, we do it hoping for relief, for happiness, for escape. Even when we hurt ourselves, we think we're helping ourselves. We call it love. We call it freedom. We call it healing. But it's just ignorance in disguise.

Self-harm is not just about pills or blades. It's when you walk into a toxic relationship thinking it's your soulmate. It's when you stay in a dead job because fear tells you it's security. It's when you binge, scroll, gossip, or obey, believing it will make you whole.

Self-harm is when you make a bad choice thinking it's a good one. It's when you act from conditioning and call it free will. It's when you follow your impulses and call it intuition.

The ancient ones called it *avidya* (ignorance). Not seeing clearly. Not knowing who you are. Not questioning what you've been told.

The worst self-harm is not a single act. It's a life lived unconsciously. It's a mind that refuses to inquire. It's a being that never asks: *Whose life am I living?*

To live as the conditioned ego is the most violent thing you can do to yourself. And the tragedy? You'll call it normal. You'll call it success. You'll even call it love.

# 10 | The Victim Card

> *The ego plays the victim to remain what it is. It prefers sympathy over solution, control over clarity."*

Just as the ego loves to claim credit, it loves to play the victim. When something good happens, it says, *I did it.* When something bad happens, it says, *It happened to me.*

Good things: I do. Bad things: happen to me. Astounding.

Playing the victim is its favorite pastime. And most of the time, it has no other option, because bad things keep happening. The ego, being what it is, rarely sees real success, so it rarely gets the chance to boast. It settles for blame instead.

The blame game is constant. One misfortune after another, and always someone else is at fault. This time, *he did it: I am the victim.* Next time, *she did it: I am again the victim.*

This is how the ego survives: by never looking at itself. By deflecting responsibility. By choosing sympathy over solution. By choosing control over clarity.

It would rather be pitied than transformed. It would rather be right than free.

# 11 | Stop Pampering the Wound

> *Hurt is the opportunity to see where you are still deluded and dependent."*

Instagram spirituality says, *The greatest religion is not to hurt others.* Search online and you get a million slogans: *The highest virtue is to never hurt anyone.*

But the fellow who gets hurt easily is already a problem to himself. Is there anyone worse? Yes, the one who pampers and mollycoddles him.

Had his hurt not been constantly patronized by friends and well-wishers, he would have dropped this tendency long ago. But we have built a culture that rewards fragility. We confuse indulgence with love.

Look at your own life. Don't we often care more for the ones who are easily hurt? Don't we rush to soothe every little complaint?

Ask simply: Is there anything apart from the ego that can be hurt? Kindly meditate on this.

We may think we are helping our loved ones by sympathizing with every injury. But most of the time, all we are doing is strengthening their bondage.

# 12 | No Belief Is Sacred

> *Spirituality is hard, unrelenting inquiry. It is philosophy with the purpose of liberation. It is not a belief system."*

Rare is the patient who openly declares: *I don't want the medicine, I love my disease.* At least he's honest in his madness.

Much more common and dangerous is the one who admits he's sick and then picks up false medicine with a knowing smile. He pretends to be healing, but is only burying the disease deeper. Such a man is not just sick, he is cunning. And his disease is now armed with deception.

This is the condition of most seekers today: spiritually diseased and deeply dishonest.

Be fiercely, unflinchingly alert against false spirituality. It wears holy robes. It chants verses. It peddles peace and promises paradise. And yet, it is just ego, dressed up in the clothes of the sacred.

Watch out for the word 'belief.' It is not harmless. It is a trap. The moment you hear yourself say, *I believe that...*, pause. Ask: *Why do I believe this? Have I seen it? Or have I borrowed it out of fear?*

Two hoots to beliefs, yours or mine. Beliefs are the wallpaper over the cracked walls of the mind.

*Everyone is entitled to their beliefs*: this is a socially acceptable lie. Legally sound, but existentially useless. Every fool has beliefs. But truth? That is another beast altogether.

Beliefs are not truth. They are psychological bandages. They protect the fragile, insecure self. They secure the ego's reign. They keep you asleep, comfortably and eternally.

So observe. When you speak with supreme confidence, when you declare, *This is how the world is. This is how things work...*, stop. Ask: *Why am I so desperate to be right? What am I afraid of losing?*

Most likely, you're clinging to a narrative that safeguards your self-image.

Anytime you hold on to something without thoroughly examining it, feel that as an alarm bell ringing in the depth of your being. You are witnessing inner foul play.

Truth does not ask for belief. It asks for burning inquiry. It demands the death of falsehood, not the decoration of it. Remember: All belief is in service of the ego. And real spirituality begins only when belief ends.

# 13 | Grow, Don't Just Glow

> "You are your most important asset. Invest wisely, and keep checking the returns."

How much should you spend on yourself? As much as it takes to extract the highest value from yourself, for yourself. Not for display, not for validation, but for real inner growth.

Sometimes, you must spend on the car: fuel, servicing, alignment. These are not indulgences; they are essentials. Without them, the car fails. You need it to take yourself to your destination, so you invest in its upkeep.

But there's another kind of spending: endlessly decorating the car with trinkets. Bejewelled dashboards, diamond-studded headlights, platinum door handles. And in the process, the fellow sold the tyres to buy the platinum knobs. Now the car looks royal, but doesn't move.

That's the story of most lives. We squander what truly matters—time, energy, attention—to acquire shiny nonsense. We invest in appearance, not essence. We polish the shell, while the engine rusts.

You are your most important asset. So ask yourself: Are you investing in movement, or in decoration?

Are you growing, or just glowing?

# 14 | Stop Defending Your Weaknesses

> *Nobody lacks strength. We merely agree to act weak for the sake of certain comforts. Strength lies in seeing that selling your spine is always a bad bargain."*

Strength is your nature. It does not need to be earned. Sounds comforting?

Here is the caveat: Strength need not be earned, but weakness must be dropped. If you have managed to stay so fragile and brittle for so long, it is only because you keep defending your weaknesses.

Look at us. We argue for our weaknesses. We decorate them, rationalize them, polish them into virtues. Are we honest with ourselves? We stand behind our frailty, and so it thrives. Why would the weak self improve if you keep accommodating it? The weak self deserves a certain disdain.

In this age of self-love slogans, it may be unfashionable to say so, but there must be a gentle disgust toward the repeated display of needless infirmity. There must be a limit to glorifying feebleness as "just being human."

Will we ever grow a spine if we remain content with crawling?

# 15 | Improvement Is Not a Strategy

> *Genuine self-improvement begins when you stop lying to yourself, see your condition as it is, and let change arise on its own."*

Self-improvement and self-deception cannot coexist. If you can't admit your inner mess, how can anything improve? How can clarity arise in a space filled with denial?

You don't always need to announce it to the world. You don't need to wear your wounds publicly. But you must confess it to yourself. You must see, without distortion, where you actually stand. That silent acknowledgment is itself transformative. It breaks the illusion. It opens the door.

When there is clarity, change happens effortlessly. Not because you force it, but because the false begins to fall away on its own.

And remember: real transformation is not aimed at some pre-decided result. It is not for fulfilling an old desire. It is not a strategy for success or happiness. It has no fixed goal. It is the spontaneous, unpredictable flowering of self-awareness.

One simply says: *I must be free of this inner mess, whatever the cost.*

No bargaining. No conditions. Just a clean, honest resolve: that's where real change begins.

# 16 | Let the Petty Go

> *If your self-worth depends on anything, life will play with it like a puppet on strings. True freedom begins when you stop measuring yourself by external yardsticks."*

Let your situations, circumstances, possessions, and particular destination in life not become significant enough to define you. Let your self-worth not be dictated by anything external.

Since everything external is fleeting, the only true freedom is to let go of the very concept of self-worth altogether.

If you hold onto a concept of self-worth, it will inevitably depend on something else, because concepts, by nature, rely on other concepts. When that something changes, your sense of self-worth will shift as well. You become a victim to the vicissitudes of life: when life lifts you up, you feel elevated; when it puts you down, you feel diminished. All this is no fun.

It is a great freedom to be relieved from carrying a sense of self-worth dependent on the world.

# 17 | Behind Your Back, Something Is Ticking

> *Don't ask how to manage time. Ask how to manage yourself."*

Your time profile is nothing but a mirror, showing you your mental profile: your actual values and priorities. Look closely at how you use your hours and minutes; they reveal what you truly hold dear.

You understand the value of time when catching a flight or a train. A missed train doesn't return. When someone dies, it hits you that time isn't eternal: it's fragile, evaporating by the second.

Yet strangely, you see yourself as the exception. Everything else may vanish, but not you. The train will leave. The flight will take off. The deadline will pass. But you? You imagine you'll remain standing forever, as if mortality doesn't apply to you. That illusion of personal timelessness is your fundamental error.

You might be young today: maybe 25, maybe 35. But if life were just three days long, one full day is already gone. That's the stark truth. Most people don't get 100 years. In practice, it's closer to 75 or 80.

So what remains? A vast canvas? No, just two days. And even they are uncertain. One is gone. Two are provisional. That's what you're working with.

If you truly grasp this, you won't keep asking how to squeeze more appointments into your calendar. You'll ask how to refine yourself. Because when you manage yourself, time follows.

# FEAR: THE INNER DICTATOR

# 18 | When the Mind Growls, Listen

> *Fear, turmoil, upsets: treat them as well-wishers. They come to whisper that something in life needs attention. Greet them honestly, and they vanish like clouds, revealing a sky that was always sunny and clear."*

If you're not feeling right, don't suppress it. Your nature is deep security and effortless rest. Anything short of complete inner stillness is a symptom. Don't ignore it. Your doubts serve a purpose. The mind's agitation is never random.

Is the mind disturbed without cause? It carries clutter because you value it. Whatever is valued will be preserved.

*Why do I value the needless?*

Because you don't know what is truly needed.

*Why don't I know what's needed?*

Because you've never known who you are. You've settled for a vague, borrowed idea, that you are a 'human being'. Rarely have you asked, with seriousness, what your true identity is.

*How do I ask that?*

## When the Mind Growls, Listen

Look at where your body, feelings, thoughts, opinions and actions arise from.

When the inner engine growls, listen. Don't pretend. What you refuse to face, you cannot repair.

# 19 | Fear Is a Liar, Test It

> *Are you afraid that something bad may happen? Fear is already the worst that can happen."*

Fear doesn't come from an event, it comes from your assumed helplessness before the event. You say you're afraid of what might happen, but are you not more afraid of how shattered you'll be if it does happen? You *assume* an impact.

Is it the event itself that terrifies you, or your own fragility in front of it? Would you still tremble if you could say with conviction: *Let anything happen. Let the world fall apart: it cannot touch what I truly am.*

If you knew yourself to be invulnerable, if you clearly saw that what is essential in you cannot be touched, altered, or taken away, would fear still have any ground to stand on?

Fear claims that the world can snatch away something precious from you. But fear is a liar. It thrives on your unexamined assumptions. Test those assumptions. Test fear itself. Let the worst come, what really happens? You'll see that even amidst collapse, you remain. Even in loss, something deeper in you stands untouched.

But there is a trap. If you have built your life around the non-essential, if your happiness is rooted in things, people, identities, and hopes, then fear will cling to you like a shadow. You will always be anxious, because you always have something to lose.

To be fearless is not to control what happens. It is to be rooted in That which cannot be lost. The key to fearlessness is not bravado, it is discernment. Drop your dependence on the trivial, and fear will drop on its own.

The world can shake only what is shaky. Know what in you is unshakable. Stand there, and be free.

# 20 | Fear Isn't Weakness, It's a Message

> *Listen to your fears,*
> *they aren't telling you where the external*
> *threat is. They are telling you where*
> *the internal work is pending."*

Fear is not your enemy. It isn't random or senseless. It comes bearing a message: *Something in you is still weak, still unexamined, still falsely built.*

Fear exposes where you're not rooted in truth. It points to the cracks you've ignored, the borrowed structures you live by. It says: here, you are not yet real.

If you don't listen, you'll keep imagining yourself as strong and sorted. Fear is the needed disruption. It humbles you. Without it, the ego floats in fantasy. You'll call yourself fearless, but in truth, you've gone deaf. You're not free, you're numb.

Fear isn't alerting you to what's outside; it's whispering about what's broken within.

You fear job interviews, not because the interviewer is dangerous, but because your self-worth is tied to approval. You fear intimacy, not because love hurts, but because your identity clings to the other.

You fear rejection, because you haven't yet found value within.

Fear reveals these inner dependencies. It shows where you're still leaning on the world, still not standing on your own ground.

Don't dismiss fear. Use it. Let it show you what needs attention: what's false, what's fragile, what must be seen and dropped.

Even the superman you pretend to be, he shivers too. And that trembling is truth knocking.

Let it in. Ask fear: *What are you here to show me?*

You'll find there's always some illusion beneath it. Something waiting to be understood. And let go.

# 21 | With Trembling Hands

> *Fearlessness is not the absence of fear. Fearlessness is freedom to not to be carried away by fear, to do the right thing in spite of fear."*

You ask: *Is it possible to act rightly with trembling hands?* I say: there is great joy in doing the right thing with trembling hands.

Often, the false path feels comfortable. It allows you to proceed smoothly, effortlessly, because it flows with the current of your inner conditioning. But Truth? Truth is a challenge. The moment you move toward it, resistance within begins to rise.

Fear, discomfort, confusion, these are not always signs of a wrong direction. In fact, more often than not, they are the marks of a genuine journey. To act rightly in spite of these inner tremors, that is strength. That is integrity.

Don't be too quick to retreat when fear appears. Let fear be. Let it tremble. Let your legs shake, your voice quiver. But don't betray the right action. The presence of fear doesn't always mean you should stop. Sometimes, it's just the ego's last attempt to keep you tied.

Understand: falseness is seductive precisely because it feels easy. It rarely offends the inner inertia. But the right thing? It will almost always demand something of you. Something real. Something costly.

So, don't drop the difficult just because it scares you. And don't hold on to the easy just because it feels safe. Comfort is no proof of rightness.

More often than not, comfort is the mask of cowardice.

If you expect the path of Truth to be smooth, you'll be discouraged too soon. Nobody—no saint, no sage, no savior—has walked the right path without stumbling. Drop the hero myths. They too had their sleepless nights.

Joy lies not in ease, but in uprightness. Not in the absence of struggle, but in not bowing to it.

So yes, trembling hands can still do the right thing. And that is the only real victory.

# 22 | The Courage to Walk Away

> *Real courage is found in battling yourself and knowing when to avoid unnecessary conflicts."*

Choose only the right battles. And once you've chosen rightly, there can be no surrender. You don't quit a battle that matters. You don't retreat from a war that defines your being.

Courage isn't about reacting to every provocation or proving strength in every situation. True courage arises only when you confront the real enemy: your own conditioning, fears, attachments, and ego.

Most problems aren't worth your energy. They are distractions in disguise. Let them pass, even if others call you weak or passive. Let them mock. Your energy is too precious to be spent on the trivial.

Not every battle is worth fighting. Often, it is wiser to bow down or walk away. Even if your silence is misunderstood. Even if you aren't seen as brave. Wisdom often wears the cloak of humility.

But when the right battle presents itself—one that touches your core and demands inner transformation—there must be no retreat. Even if it costs you everything, you stand.

That is courage.

## 23 | Confidence Is Fear

> *The more dependent you are, the more afraid you will be. The key to fearlessness is not confidence, it is freedom.*

Confidence doesn't cure fear, it only masks it. Like a pill, it offers temporary relief but leaves the disease untouched. Fear remains, silently breeding underneath. Don't medicate fear. Understand it.

Fearlessness isn't about standing tall with clenched fists. It's about not needing to stand tall for anyone. When there's nothing to lose, what is there to fear?

As long as your mind values what it gets from the world—approval, validation, identity—you will remain afraid. When the world lives inside you, it controls you. And when it controls you, it haunts you.

You don't fear people or situations. You fear the damage they might do to your self-image, your sense of worth. That is dependency.

The more occupied you are with others—what they say, how they look, what they might take—the more hollow you become within. Fear is not weakness. It's a signal: your inner space is cluttered.

## Confidence Is Fear

Fear feeds on this inner occupation. And from that fear arises the craving for confidence. Not as strength, but as a disguise. The more afraid you are, the more confident you try to appear. But appearance isn't peace. Performance isn't freedom.

Confidence is not the opposite of fear, rather it is the accompanying shadow of fear.

Don't ask how to gain confidence. Ask: why do I even need it?

When your insides are clean, when your mind is no longer a dumping ground for the world's expectations, you don't crave confidence. You don't need it.

Your inner space must be your sanctum sanctorum. Let the world remain outside. Within, there must be silence. Clarity. Purity untouched by praise or blame.

Here is the mantra:

Whenever you feel fear, trembling, or even hope in the presence of the other—be it a person, object, or situation—remind yourself: *I am feeling this only because I am being dependent. I need not depend. I am free.*

All fear arises from dependency. Don't use shallow confidence to fight deep fear. Use fear to spot dependency: that is the beginning of the end of ignorance, and therefore, of fear.

# 24 | Fear Never Comes as Fear

> *Your real oppressor is not the other. You are oppressed by your own inner fear, greed, insecurity and ignorance."*

We keep blaming society, systems, and circumstances. But look closely: is it really the other who binds you, or your own urge to conform, to please, to belong, to secure?

Fear is when you're told you must marry to avoid loneliness in old age. You don't seek companionship: you seek insurance.

Fear is when you accept a job you dislike because the perks make it look respectable.

Fear is when you buy life insurance, not out of understanding, but because the world warns you that death must be "prepared for."

Fear is when you marry your girlfriend because society wants the relationship legalized.

Fear is when you don't marry her because society objects to caste.

Fear is when you obey tradition, not because it is wise, but because disobedience feels dangerous.

Don't you see how fear disguises itself? It shows up as love, duty, career, responsibility, maturity. Fear never announces itself. It hides beneath what is culturally celebrated.

## Fear Never Comes as Fear

You follow. Not because you are weak, but because you have never investigated your uneasiness. You feel something is off, yet you silence that inner discomfort. You call it compromise. You call it adulthood.

But that uneasiness is your clue. Don't dismiss it. It is sacred. It is the whisper of Truth, telling you something is false. Something isn't yours.

Pay attention. Not reaction. Not rationalization. Just attention.

Attention will reveal how fear and greed have quietly taken over. While you keep blaming others, the real ruler sits inside your own mind.

Your family, your boss, your religion, your government, none of them have the power to truly oppress you unless fear within you is already cooperating with them.

And fear within doesn't scream. It seduces. It smiles. It pretends to care. It tells you to be safe, to play along, to not make trouble.

Name it. Expose it. Refuse to bow before it.

The real revolution does not begin on the street. It begins in the mirror.

# 25 | The Next Step Is Enough

> *True action doesn't flow from ambition, it flows from inner clarity. It doesn't need maps, just the next right step."*

We often deceive ourselves. We coast on convenience, rest in excuses, and wrap ourselves in the illusion that we're already trying hard enough. But the truth is sobering: we don't challenge ourselves enough. We don't stretch to the brink. We don't ruthlessly use our tragically limited, fleeting resources. Yet we sit, hoping and praying for a miracle, for some divine helping hand to descend and rescue us.

It won't.

And that's the most liberating news: no help is coming, because none is needed. Even in confusion and fear, you already have enough to take the next step. You are not helpless. You're just outsourcing your responsibility.

The path is veiled. You don't see the peak. You don't know what lies beyond the bend. But who does? Nobody is ever given the full map. What you are given, always, is the power to take the next right step. And that is all that's ever required.

## The Next Step Is Enough

Take that step with intensity and full-hearted commitment. Life doesn't ask for perfection or omniscience, it asks for just one honest step into the unknown, aligned with the right.

What comes after that? That's none of your business. Truth does not reveal itself to the idle thinker or the anxious planner. It reveals itself only to the one who walks toward it without guarantees. It reveals itself often not as something to achieve or something to go toward, but as something to liberate yourself from.

Forget your goals. They are usually just conditioned desires of the ego. Instead, ask: *What is the right action now?* Let that question pierce you. Let that be your compass.

You don't need more time. You don't need more resources. You need more honesty.

Take the next step. That alone is your redemption.

What after the next? We said that's not our business to ask.

# THE HUNGER THAT CONSUMES

# 26 | The Punishment Called Entertainment

> *You are looking for entertainment because you are deeply bored. Find out what is worthy of devoting your entire life to!*

Why do we see ordinary people, and worse still, vicious ones, enjoying life? Why are the courageous often seen in pain? Why do thinkers look serious, while the average Joe is giggling?

What we normally call enjoyment is just a kind of entertainment or titillation. Such titillation any wretched fellow can have, and that itself is the punishment.

If one is chasing entertainment, if one craves a lot of excitement, that itself is the punishment.

Why does one desperately need unending fun? Why is life devoid of the simple thrill of right living? Isn't there elation in overcoming fear? Isn't there exhilaration in a fresh discovery? Isn't love ecstatic? If yes, then why do most people need an extra dose of fun, also known as dopamine?

Why are all the shopping malls overflowing on the weekend? Maybe because people have had a pathetic week. When you have a pathetic week, then you require a sensational weekend.

# The Punishment Called Entertainment

Such entertainment is just punishment for putting up with a rotten week. Why tolerate a bad job for five days? So that the money it gives you can be consumed on the weekend? Doesn't look like a good deal.

# 27 | Eh! Go, Get a Life

> *The world is really owned*
> *by the innocent man who finds*
> *a playground and a dancefloor everywhere.*
> *The world is ruled by the joyful,*
> *secure insider who is at home everywhere.*
> *The rest are all fooling themselves and missing*
> *the game."*

There was a kids' learning camp I conducted in the Himalayas, all five-to eight-year-olds. Among other things, I bought three or four masks, really scary masks, as per me. I also bought a couple of rubber snakes and a menacing dragon.

With the kids asleep one early morning, I sneaked up to them, brandishing the masks and flaunting the snakes. The masks threatened, and the snakes duly hissed. One of the kids lazily opened just one eye, threw a contemptuous glance at me—as one does at a witless buffoon—and turning over, resumed her sleep, her nonchalance dismissing me with: *Eh! Go, get a life.*

I felt hurt!

But she had taught me something:

When the world comes to you with all its bullying faces, simply say, "Eh?" and go back to sleep.

There is really no pleasure deeper than not getting affected when the clowns are all conspiring to unsettle you. This deepest pleasure is called *Joy*.

Think: everybody, the entire game of situations, seems dead set on freaking you out, on just destroying your peace, and you are looking at it with indifference: *Yes? Do I know you?*

Don't even acknowledge them. They are not worth even your disapproval.

The fellow is dancing a terrible dance, hoping to extract some reaction from you, and the greatest reaction is that you start snoring.

You are home. Casually. Innocently. Like a sleepy kid secure in existence's arms.

# 28 | You Invited the Thief

> *First your desires open the gate to your exploitation. Only then others enter and exploit you. Blaming others won't help, close the door."*

You have a burning need. You badly want something. Word spreads. And suddenly, all kinds of vendors show up, not to help, but to profit from your desperation.

A needy customer is a seller's dream. And when the buyer is impatient, the seller knows he can promise anything, deliver nothing, and still succeed. He brings you spurious goods, hollow comforts, and you take them. Why? Because you can't bear your emptiness. You want escape, not understanding.

This is how the world exploits you. You have a void inside, and instead of watching it quietly, you cry out. The world hears your cry, and offers counterfeit solutions. And later you say: *They fooled me.* No, they didn't. You exposed yourself. They merely entered the door you left open.

When the world sees your desperation for peace, love, or meaning, it rushes in with noise. The more restless you are, the more you fall.

But the moment you stop needing, the game changes. You can now assess, question, wait. You say: *Let me see what you offer.* You are no longer a helpless buyer. You are someone with clarity, and that's what the market fears most.

The world exploits only the unexamined. Observe your own hunger, and the vultures lose power. They thrive only when you are blind to your inner chaos.

Others can exploit you only after you've first abandoned yourself. If you don't want to be deceived, stop being needy. If you don't want to be sold lies, stop begging for comfort.

You're not helpless. But clarity begins with one simple act: close the door.

# 29 | Distractions Don't Win, Weak Goals Lose

> *If you choose a goal not worthy enough, it makes no sense to stay concentrated on it."*

If the goal doesn't grip you, the world will. Distractions don't win; your goal simply fails to hold you.

If you keep struggling to concentrate, don't ask why you're distracted, ask why the goal is so lifeless. A weak aim invites the mind to wander. If you must repeatedly remind yourself to focus, it means your heart isn't in it. Distraction isn't the problem, it's the symptom.

Let the goal be so compelling that it shields you. You don't protect it. It protects you. A worthy goal absorbs you. It doesn't ask for discipline; it becomes breath, movement, music. In its presence, distractions lose meaning. They seem silly, colourless, beneath you.

But look at how goals are usually chosen. Most are inherited or imposed—by family, culture, media, peers. Such goals aren't your beloveds; they're your chains. Obviously, you feel bored and the mind escapes. And then you blame yourself for lacking will. But the fault lies in the fake goal, not in your being.

Concentration is needed only where there is resistance. When the act is joyful, focus happens on its own. When you are in love, do you need to force yourself to stay? When work flows from your essence, it is not work, it is meditation.

Desire needs effort. Because desire wants to reach somewhere else, it stays restless, split, unsure. Love asks for nothing. It flows for the sake of flowing. It enjoys itself. It is the reward.

The world doesn't steal you. You leave yourself when you chase what you don't love. Then you accuse the world of tempting you away.

Don't try to fight distractions. Don't aim to improve concentration. Let love be your choice, let love set your goals. Love enjoys dissolution, and laughs at both distraction and concentration.

# 30 | No Trophies, Just Play

> *Complete within, you do not repeatedly turn to the world begging for companionship. Complete within, you do not even have anything against the world. Complete within, you are free to engage in energetic action, vigorous doing, without having a particular fruit in mind."*

We say life needs a motive, a driver. But does that driver have to be a constant sense of smallness and inferiority?

So much of life is spent in the pursuit of amassing something in order to get bigger and better. But have we questioned the belief that we are inherently incomplete and insufficient?

That belief is ingrained deep into our mind. Where did it come from? It seems the most fundamental idea implanted into us since birth. Family, education, media, culture, each has told us to accumulate stuff and security from the world before we can be deemed successful.

It is wonderful to have material goals and chase them, provided you are not seeking fundamental inner fulfilment from those goals.

When you start from a point of completeness, all your actions and ambitions carry the flavour of completeness. When you act out of the sheer joy of being, the results become irrelevant from an inner standpoint.

Externally, you might be defined by possessions or successes. Internally, you must remain complete, irrespective of the state of your body, mind, bank balance, or reputation.

Externally, there will be successes and failures. Internally, there can be failure only when there is psychological dependency on the result of effort.

When your internal identity is on the line, only then does an adverse external outcome feel like an inner failure. There can be no failure when you begin from a point of unreasonable sureness: you are already successful.

Your true identity does not depend on any achievement or situation outside of yourself. The world is a playground, good for merriment, but with no real trophies to be won.

Now, go play, fearlessly.

# 31 | Before You Win, Ask: What Are You Winning?

> *All your successes are meaningless if your goal itself is unwise."*

Success does not lie in doing any random thing just to fulfill a blind desire, or worse, to please a crowd. You must know who you are and what you really need.

Victory lies first in choosing the right battle to fight. If you fight the wrong battle, isn't victory worse than defeat? There is no success in chasing a foolish goal and managing to attain it. If the goal itself is unworthy, what glory is there in attaining it more speedily than others?

So, do not ask: *How do I get success in whatever I do?* By asking in such terms, you are trivializing action. 'Whatever' in your question is a gaping wound. Close it. One does not do 'whatever'. Much more thought, much more consideration, must go into what is worthy of being done.

Only two types of actions are worth it: one, that arises from your inner fulfillment, the very dance of joy. And two, that which takes you toward fulfillment: the courage of love, the light of wisdom.

So, pause, reflect, take your time. Be open, alert, and inquisitive. Life is precious. Time is not to be squandered chasing unworthy goals.

# 32 | The Myth of Free Time

> *Life deserves purpose and passion. True freedom is found in meaningful work, not empty idleness."*

The surest way to squander time is by engaging oneself emotionally in some little thing, thinking continuously and remaining wastefully embroiled.

Life means time, every second is precious. One is born in the bondage of physical tendencies, and one grows up to gather more bondages from society and influences. The purpose of life is to unlearn as much as you can, refine yourself as much as you can, and liberate yourself as much as you can. Like the branches of a mighty tree, grow freely in all possible directions, contemptuous of everything that tries to keep you in limits.

Don't allow time to just pass by. Hold the moment by the scruff and extract the maximum value. You shouldn't have even a second of the so-called 'free time'—sounds strange, but please think about it. All your time must be occupied in liberative, loving, courageous endeavours.

One somehow completes his daily tasks, returns to his place, slumps on the couch and says: *Now, this is my free time. Where is the TV remote?* This is not free time. This is bondage time.

## The Myth of Free Time

The word 'free' is a sacred word; it cannot be used casually. What does one mean by 'free'? Free of what?

Real freedom is freedom from our internal bondages. So what is free time, then? Time spent in pursuit of freedom: only such time deserves to be called free time. Otherwise, the free time that we normally give ourselves is just toxic. Nothing does us greater disservice than this so-called free time.

Think of all the nonsense that people do in their free time. In fact, most nonsense gets done only in free time. Think of what people need free time for. For great activities? For stuff that liberates the mind, elevates the consciousness? Well, quite the contrary.

Time is to be spent in pursuit of the highest that life can give you. In the real sense, only such a liberative pursuit can be called work. Work is not just the putting together of a career and a livelihood.

Life is short. There is sacred work to do, a free place to reach. When your action carries all your love for freedom, all your truth, your total sincerity, only then you should say: *This is my free time.*

Free time isn't about freedom from work. Free time is when you work the hardest in love of freedom.

# 33 | Nothing Lasts but the Joke

> *Don't accord the status of Beyond to anything. Everything is dispensable. Nothing here is permanent or indestructible, don't raise futile hopes. Live in good-humored contempt toward the world, and obviously yourself! Treat it all as a bit of a joke."*

Show me anything that is really the way you think of it.

Show me something that remains tomorrow as it is today.

Show me something that doesn't belie your expectations.

The wise person does not let impermanencies get too big on him. She knows the game of situations: today this thing, tomorrow something else. These things are not loyal to anybody; they are not committed to anybody; they will not stand by anybody. They are fleeting, impermanent, will-o'-the-wisp kinds.

Seen carefully, all that is seen is impermanence. Stability is a mirage we rely on. The mature mind does not give too much weightage to the impermanent, at least it does not allow the impermanent to disguise as unchanging and dependable.

Things are things, thoughts are thoughts, and people are people, all ever-changing. They will not fulfill your craving for stability and security, just as a sequence of food items on a cinema screen can't satisfy your hunger.

We have a stake in imagining objects to be unchanging, permanent, and hence dependable. We want to feel secure by clinging to reliable objects. Hence we deliberately ignore the impermanent fact of things and imagine them to be frozen in time.

Isn't this self-deception?

To expect things to be as per your image of them is to invite suffering.

# 34 | Joy: The Hardest Pleasure

*The joy of overcoming yourself is much deeper and more authentic than the fleeting pleasure of indulging yourself."*

Joy is not ordinary pleasure, not ordinary happiness; it takes you higher. But it is a very demanding and exacting pleasure.

The lowly kinds of pleasures are cheap, you can get them easily: go sell yourself, get drunk, crash in a brothel. Lowly pleasures are yours for the taking. Go binge and pass out.

Most of our pleasures degrade us. But equally, one cannot live without pleasure. Let us then choose the higher kind of pleasure, one that comes with elevation of consciousness.

Such elevating pleasure is a difficult one. The wise ones have given it a special name to differentiate it from ordinary pleasure: joy.

The right pleasure is difficult, hence we opt for lowly pleasures. If you think you are doing something right in life and yet there isn't a difficult joy, then you are mistaken.

Most of the time, our default inner movement comes from the wrong centre. The right movement? You have to be very careful about. It is a sensitive, delicate thing; it has to be crafted, it has to be engineered with all your intelligence and devotion.

## Joy: The Hardest Pleasure

In contrast, the default thing is like freefall in gravity: it just happens.

What does it take to fly an airplane at 35,000 feet? Generations of engineering.

What does it take for a plane to crash? Nothing, one drunk pilot and the plane is gone.

It is always easier to fall. Go for the right kind of pleasure.

Wisdom is about having great pleasures. Love is about attempting the highest flight, the kind that normal people do not even think of.

# 35 | Your Goals Are Not Yours

> *There is no wave in the mind that arises on its own. The mind is dependent on the world, and the world is dependent on the mind.*"

What is the goal for a terrorist?

Kill.

What is the goal for a Hindu?

Temple.

What is the goal for a Muslim?

Mosque.

What is the goal for a fly?

Dirt and rubbish.

What is the goal for a hormone-driven body?

Physical pleasure.

What is the goal for a greedy mind?

Money.

What is the goal for a bored mind?

Entertainment.

What is the goal for a dependent mind?

Social acceptance.

What is the goal for an insecure mind?

A support.

What is the goal that the mind chases?

That which it is conditioned to chase.

What is the mind?

A random compilation of stuff that the ego has mistakenly accumulated.

# 36 | Sex Isn't the Problem, Emptiness Is

> *Isn't sexual obsession a symptom of inner emptiness? When you know who you are, sex ceases to be an unconscious, uncontrollable mental urge. Sex is simple and biological, obsession is complex and mental.*

Understand your desire. You must know what you are really hungry for. Your central and primary desire is not sex. Sex may appear overpowering and promise to be deeply fulfilling, but it doesn't really deliver the goods.

We live without self-awareness. Our obsession with sex is one of the fallouts. If one can figure out what one really must have, then sex will automatically, inwardly, be assigned its proper place. It would remain neither a thing to be coveted, nor a thing to be condemned.

For most of us, sex is not just a biological activity. To us, sex carries magnificent notions: the lure of ultimate fulfillment.

We are a hyper-sexualized species and society. Because we do not have inner fulfillment, we place mega-emphasis on one ordinary aspect of our biological being: sex. We have expectations from all kinds of material, and we harbour the maximum expectation from the material body.

In some sense, great sexual urge is an indicator of great inner energy waiting to find the right direction. Give it the right direction.

How?

Begin by realising, confronting, and acknowledging the worthlessness of your current direction.

# 37 | The Final Cure for Addiction

> "Addictions arise from an inner void. And the only way to break free is to fill that space with something higher, something truly meaningful."

Addictions exist to plug a deep inner hollow. You must first acknowledge the fact of your addiction. You do feel, perhaps unconsciously, that these things are doing you some good. Otherwise, why would you keep returning to them?

Addictions exist because, at some level, you have nothing better. At least that's what the inner animal believes. It doesn't understand, it only feels.

There's no point cursing the objects of addiction. They didn't beg to enter your life. You went to them, eager, needy and drooling. Be it TV shows, social media, porn, relationships, money, drugs: they are not the problem. Your need for them is.

Why are you going to them? That's where self-knowledge begins. Look within. You go to them because there's a crying hollow inside. And unless you bring something higher into your life, that hollow will keep sucking you back, no matter how much you rage against it.

# The Final Cure for Addiction

Bring something into your life that is bigger than your cravings. Something you know is worth more than the cheap thrills.

I refuse to believe that a young person of intelligence and sensitivity cannot think of something nobler to pursue. Set your mind on something high, something beautiful and you'll find you no longer have time for the petty.

Your attention will become razor-sharp. You'll know what matters. And you won't want to look elsewhere.

What you call distractions or addictions are just symptoms of purposelessness. You cannot be addicted unless you are empty. Fall in love with a purpose, and the nonsense will vanish like mist in sunlight.

You don't need counseling. You need a question: What is the highest you can think of? What is the most beautiful you can imagine? And why is it not worth giving your life to?

# 38 | Keep the Man Aside

> *The man should not be at the center of the woman's world, and vice versa. Such a thing belongs to the jungle. Humanness begins only when you leave the jungle behind."*

The body, the hormones, the maternity, the nest: as long as these remain the nucleus of a woman's life, there can be no real liberation. And when her body stops being her master, the man too will stop being her obsession.

Exactly the same applies in reverse to men. But for now, let's talk about dear ladies.

If you find that a person has become too important to you, pause and ask: *Is this importance arising from love or just dependence?* Most of the time, it is dependence masquerading as devotion. You see the evidence in a glaring disparity: the woman may or may not be the center of a man's world, but far more often, the man becomes the center of the woman's world. This lopsided equation is a source of chronic stress for both.

The undue importance the woman has been taught to her body, her biology, the nest, and the man—these are not separate; they are one tangled complex. Freedom for the woman from her body is freedom from the man. And freedom for the woman inevitably means freedom for the man as well. Similarly, freedom for the man means freedom for the woman as well.

No person, thing or thought can be the centre of your universe. Attainment of your highest inner potential is what you are born for. Pursuing big desires, while remaining small, is pointless. The relentless resolve to not to remain small is self-attainment.

Freedom begins the moment you stop begging another to complete you. Only in freedom can there be dignity, and love.

# 39 | Beyond Happiness

> *You must remember that the goal of life is not happiness, but freedom from the tension to obtain happiness."*

What is the ultimate purpose of life? Earning money? Chasing happiness? How can something so shallow, so petty, be the grand purpose of existence?

The happiness you know has two fatal flaws. First, it is merely a product of conditioning. You have been trained to call certain fleeting excitements 'happiness.' Second, it exists only in contrast to sadness.

So if you want to be happy, you must first be sad. If you want deep happiness, be prepared to become deeply miserable first. That is the hidden absurdity of it all.

Joy is something entirely different. Joy is reasonless. Joy is uncaused. Joy is not a reaction. It is your very nature, waiting to be uncovered.

Only the one whose mind is not buried under a thousand layers of conditioning can know love. Only that one can know joy.

The free one is free from sadness. And equally free from the craving for happiness.

She does not chase pleasure. She does not run from pain. She is light. She sees. She understands. Wow, is that not love?

And is that not the purpose of life? Simple. Clear. Unmistakable.

# 40 | The Earth Burns because You Do

> "Man's hunger is not in the stomach. It resides in the mind. That hunger—blind, restless, insatiable—has destroyed everything it could touch. Climate change is only the latest, the most devastating, and perhaps the final symptom of this inner disease."

You cannot live wrongly and hope to consume rightly. Right life and right coexistence with the Earth go together.

And what is the right life?

It begins with a simple fact: to be alive is to be conscious. And consciousness means to know. Of all that can be known, the knower is the most important. Before knowing the world, the knower must first know herself. This is self-knowledge: awareness of one's thoughts, feelings, impulses, and their relation to the world.

When this inward gaze arises, life straightens itself. Right action follows. When you live consciously, you live cleanly. You do not need a sustainability manual. Your carbon footprint falls not by design but by default.

Today, our endless emissions—carbon dioxide, methane, oxides of sulphur and nitrogen—are not just environmental pollutants. They are inner symptoms. The Earth is being destroyed by our ignorance, not by our machines. One who cuts forests is already hollow within. One who poisons rivers has already lost clarity. One who pollutes the air is already burning inside. Environmental collapse is the outer face of inner darkness. Man, like every organism, is entitled to interact with nature. But how much can he extract and consume? And how many can do that?

If eight billion, soon to be eleven, aspire to consume like Americans or Germans, collapse is not a question of if, only when.

We need to be fewer. And we need to consume with an intelligent eye on our true welfare. Ask yourself: *Do I really need that third car? What did the first two give me? What do I still lack that the third will fix?*

These are not moral questions. They are questions of clarity. Of survival.

If you live with awareness, you will consume wisely. No treaties or laws will be needed. But if you live unconsciously, then no legislation will help. Whereas when we lead a life that is honestly self-aware, we find that our carbon footprint automatically reduces, even without planning.

Governments are elected by the very people destroying the planet. If the masses are blind, their leaders cannot have sight. You cannot expect conscious legislation from an unconscious population.

Summits won't save us. Treaties won't stop the fire. No law can fix what the individual refuses to see.

Governments follow the will of the people. And the people want more: more comfort, more convenience, more consumption. No government can go too far against its voters. So, if the individual remains asleep, the system will remain broken.

The solution is not political. It is personal. The change must begin within.

## The Earth Burns because You Do

This is not a sermon. This is not moralism. This is clarity. This is realism. This is the voice of a planet that is running out of time, the cry of the ground that is burning beneath our feet.

# 41 | Don't Kill Desire. Purify It.

> *It's not the desire or attachment that is wrong, but the object you have chosen to be attached to. Let your longing be for the Truth, and it will carry you to liberation."*

Desire is not your enemy. Attachment is not your downfall. The problem is not that you chase, it's what you chase. The illness lies not in wanting, but in wanting wrongly.

Desire, attraction, ambition, drive, these are not sins. They are sacred faculties of the mind. But they become dangerous, even demonic, when misdirected, when wasted on what is petty, fleeting, false.

Don't kill your longing. That would be spiritual suicide. Redeem it. Purify it. Let your attraction be for the Truth. Let your attachment be to that which liberates.

These inner forces are not accidents, they are instruments. If you couldn't desire, how would you ever love? If you weren't drawn, how would you ever move?

The crisis is not that you are attached. The crisis is that you're attached to the unworthy, the unreal, the untrue. You chase mirages, cling to shadows, worship idols of pleasure and validation, and then wonder why life feels hollow.

So be desirous. Be fiercely attached. Be devoted. But only to the Highest. To that which calls you beyond yourself. Be drawn to those who reflect the Truth. Be attached to what dismantles your falseness.

Freedom doesn't mean feeling nothing. It means feeling rightly. Let your desire burn bright, so bright it burns away everything false.

# WORK, WILL, AND THE RIGHT FIGHT

# 42 | Continuity, Not Perfection

> *Fight an impossibly high battle. Be your own hero.*"

First, before you enter the arena, be clear what life is and what truly matters. Set high standards. And then live up to them.

If you must fail a hundred times in the right attempt, or pay a heavy price, so be it. That is the cost of living with depth.

Do not expect ease. Do not expect applause. The path of integrity is not meant to comfort you. You will stumble. You may fall. Still, persist.

Keep fighting, as naturally as you breathe, and till you breathe. More importantly, keep fighting even in defeat.

Keep going when the blow has landed.

Keep going when the score reads against you.

Keep going when the world says: *It's over.*

Fight when your strength is gone.

Fight when your cause looks foolish or forgotten. Fight when no one stands beside you, when even memory seems to have abandoned you.

Don't collapse into self-pity. Don't spiral into guilt.

*Oh, I betrayed my sacred cause by failing!*

No, you didn't.

You did what you could, in that moment.

And now, do what is still possible. What remains.

That is the essence: continuity.

Not glamour, not perfection. Just a clean, humble continuity.

Let the world think the battle is over. Let them celebrate. Even if the scoreboard says they've won, they haven't, if you haven't yet conceded defeat.

Because this is not about winning in worldly terms. This is about not turning away from what is right.

# 43 | From One Fire to the Next

> *Find out what is it that you can do even without being paid for it. That's the trick. Can I do something in just love? Can I allow that love to become my life?"*

The body wants goals that can be ticked off a list, goals that promise results, rewards, recognition. But consciousness is in search of something else, something so worthy, so luminous, that even if you chase it forever, you will never fully claim it.

That is why you must be madly in love with what you choose to do. Or better yet, do something so vast, so challenging, that love becomes inevitable.

Remember, the ultimate goal is within. It is the annihilation of all inner darkness and all bondage. But because this goal is inward, it cannot be attacked head-on. So you pick a series of outer projects, bold and demanding, that keep dissolving your inner ignorance bit by bit.

Externally, every project will begin and end. You will complete one, and you will feel tempted to rest. Do not. The work is never over. Each victory must immediately point you to the next challenge. What that will be, you will know only when you have crossed the current one.

Real success is not a single accomplishment. It is the refusal to stagnate. It is the lifelong movement into deeper clarity, deeper surrender, deeper freedom.

If you can keep turning inward, if you can keep choosing the most demanding love over the most convenient comfort, you are already victorious.

# 44 | Beat Yourself

> *The most heroic of all battles is the one you fight against yourself. Be a winner! Beat yourself!"*

We have desires, and we face threats to our interests. Life is an unending battle, always challenging, and potentially delightful.

Often, the inability to respond rightly to life's problems feels like defeat. These defeats baffle and hurt. We wonder why we can't live as winners.

If we honestly observe, we find that more than any external factor, our defeats arise from our own lack of discretion and determination.

What causes indiscretion? And what makes us lose resolve and surrender to challenges?

Here are a few pointers: Have we seen how bodily composition dictates us? How the actions and reactions of hormones, glands, and brain chemicals rule our thoughts, feelings, and behaviour? The body is primitive, and we seem hardwired to react primitively to situations. That's where our defeats start. If we can see that clearly, won't our vulnerability to challenges reduce?

Similarly, have we seen how deeply we are conditioned by upbringing, religion, education, media, and the narratives told to us?

The real enemy may be within us, in the form of our biological impulses and social conditioning. So, there is no point fighting the wrong battle. Once we see how the human being is a conditioned machine, designed to obey certain masters, then there is a possibility to stop the compulsive obedience, and live in freedom.

That is victory.

# 45 | Deadlines to Discipline to Freedom

> *Embrace deadlines today,*
> *so one day, you may rise beyond*
> *the need for them."*

When you are truly mature and independent, you don't need deadlines. You do what must be done, simply because it must be done.

But if you aren't there yet, then love deadlines. Don't resent them, welcome them. Because they help you walk the path of discipline and clarity.

A deadline is needed only when you operate within a structure: an educational setup, a corporate system, or a correctional framework. Its presence simply reveals: you are not yet internally aligned enough to act without outer pressure.

So, the first thing is to acknowledge that. Admit it honestly: *I don't yet love this enough to do it without being told.* If that love were present, no deadline would be needed.

Deadlines exist because without them, you would delay, you would escape, you would procrastinate. So instead of resenting them, feel some gratitude: *Had this deadline not been there, I wouldn't have done half of what I've managed.*

## Deadlines to Discipline to Freedom

If you reflect deeply, you'll see that much of your learning, perhaps ninety percent, has come via deadlines. That exam you studied for, that project you completed, that speech you prepared: each was a deadline in disguise, and each one shaped you.

Translate 'deadline' into 'discipline'. And see what discipline really is. Discipline comes from the same root as disciple. A disciple is one who is eager to learn. One who stays close to the teacher.

So, when you respect a deadline, you become a student. And when you become a student, you begin to learn. And when you truly begin to learn, something beautiful happens: you start enjoying deadlines.

Eventually, the day comes when deadlines dissolve. Not because you reject them, but because they are no longer needed. You become your own teacher. You learn out of love, not fear. You act from clarity, not compulsion.

That is real freedom.

# 46 | Win Small, Win Often

> *Greatness lies not in being supercapable or superhuman. Greatness lies in exceeding your capabilities, in fighting your limits."*

To be alive is to be embattled, isn't it? Struggle permeates every aspect of living. But you don't have to dwell on the final victory. That ultimate triumph in life, if it comes, will be a gift beyond imagination, not something to obsess over.

What truly matters are your daily battles: the small, quiet victories you earn each day. Chasing the grand prize brings only brief excitement, followed by exhaustion and disappointment. It drains more than it drives.

Instead, go to bed each night as a fighter. Wake knowing what battles await. Never retire without giving them your fiercest, cleanest effort. That exhaustion spent in honest struggle, that is victory.

Practice winning, not in the eyes of the world, but in your own. Practice overcoming your inertia. That takes love: for yourself, and for what is right. Defeat is not the outcome. Defeat is holding back. Defeat is when you don't fully rise to meet what the moment asks of you.

So win small. Win often. Win continuously.

# 47 | The Joy of Right Action

> *Choose the right option, make the right decision, fight the right battle—and now it doesn't matter whether you win. Victorious you already are."*

Victory is not an external prize. It is your inner alignment with what you know to be right in your clearest self.

When your decision is clean, when your choice is inwardly just, the outcome loses central relevance. What matters then is: you stood where you must. And once you're standing there, the question of success or failure doesn't bother beyond a point.

Do the utmost that life demands in any situation, without holding back. Then there is no grief, no regret. Only the joy of right action. A joy that comes not from applause, but from clarity.

Wails and tears are for those who default. Who delay, negotiate, avoid. They cry later because they didn't show up fully when it counted.

If you are truly fulfilling your responsibility, it will consume you. It will take your last ounce of energy, your final drop of stamina. There will be no fuel left to mourn, no space left for regret.

## The Joy of Right Action

If you still find yourself lamenting, look again. Some effort was held back. A reserve was kept aside for guilt, for indulgence.

Commitment means this: not just fighting the right battle, but being so fully surrendered to it that even defeat cannot distract you.

# 48 | Fill Your Life, or It Will Fill Itself

> *A purposeless life doesn't stay empty: it gets occupied by noise."*

If you will not fill your life with highness, with joy, with understanding, with beauty and purity, the result is that your life will fill itself—with rubbish.

Sometimes that rubbish is in the form of a job, sometimes a relationship, at other times something else.

Don't let that happen to you.

Man is not born into leisure. He is born into struggle. His life is a battlefield, from beginning to end. He must face challenges.

But which challenges? That is the only choice he must make.

You could spend your entire life entangled in dozens of petty distractions: silly fights, shallow dilemmas, ego-driven competitions. These are not real wars. Skirmishes. Squabbles. Fuss. They drain you, but they don't lift you.

Or, you could dedicate your life to one real battle, the central and worthy project: awakening, clarity, Truth.

If that singular commitment is absent, your energies will find other outlets, automatic and unworthy ones. Instead of rising into focus, they will scatter in every direction.

## Fill Your Life, or It Will Fill Itself

A thousand leaks.

And you won't even notice it while it's happening. You will feel 'busy,' even 'engaged.' But that is not the same as being devoted.

Your life will slowly bleed away. Not like a man who falls to a single sword, but like one who dies from a thousand small cuts.

# 49 | Impossible Is the Invitation

> *"There's no space for despair or self-pity when you're fully occupied with what must be done."*

Even in moments that appear utterly hopeless, if every fiber of your being is devoted to doing what is possible, can there really be any space left for sorrow?

When you give yourself entirely to what must be addressed, where is the time for indulgence? Where is the mind left to manufacture despair?

In truth, the more overwhelming the situation, the less luxury it offers to collapse into suffering. If the enemy surrounds you two thousand to one, can you afford to retreat into a corner and weep over your fate? There is simply no room for such dramatics.

A crushing situation is not an invitation to mourn, it is a summons to act. Its sheer intensity forces you to be fully present. Your energy, your attention, your entire being is compelled to meet the moment. The ego has no space to run its petty routines.

Give your utmost. Choose rightly, and offer your full presence to your choice. Then you begin to know a different kind of joy: not one born of results, but of pure engagement. Not comfort, but clarity.

Know yourself well, so you clearly know what you're responsible for. Self-awareness makes irresponsibility impossible.

Suffering, in the end, belongs only to those who abandon their responsibility.

Despair is not the fruit of external events, it is the mark of inner negligence.

# 50 | Loveless Work Is Joyless Life

*If your work is not lovable, life won't be liveable."*

Work is not just a compartment in your daily schedule. It is the most dominant, most identity-defining aspect of your life. Your days revolve around it, your thoughts are shaped by it, and your relationships are influenced by it. To disregard the significance of work is to ignore a central axis of your existence.

That's why I've always urged those standing at a career crossroads: never allow a discord to arise between who you are and what you do. If your work demands that you compromise on your values, then every paycheck becomes a quiet betrayal of your self. If you live divided, you will live discontent.

Your work is not some external machinery you operate, it is a mirror. It reflects your inner constitution. Don't fool yourself by saying: *I work only for money. My real life begins after office hours.* There is no such division. You are one indivisible consciousness. And every hour at work either honors that truth or erodes it.

Can you truly be a gentle, loving father to your children, and yet labor for a company that slaughters innocent animal babies to sell packaged meat? Is your compassion limited to your home? Is your integrity a weekend project? Let that contradiction haunt you, until it is resolved.

## Loveless Work Is Joyless Life

Let your actions express your true nature. Let the one who acts be indistinguishable from the truth they claim to live by. There must be no mask between what you are and how you work.

Because if you do not love your work, you will find it hard, perhaps impossible, to love your life.

## 51 | The Battle Worth Fighting

> *Fight the right battle, and only the right battle.*"

Let's honestly acknowledge a difficult truth: for most of us, a big part of life has been spent on trivial pursuits and undue attachment to fleeting things. That's how the years kept passing by.

If we look back, it becomes difficult to explain what the various decades of life went into. These affairs were not important, and consequently, they took little inner muscle to fight. One's fortitude, resolve, and courage were neither needed nor awakened in dealing with frivolous stuff.

And then grace shines through, often in the form of a deeply important battle one unexpectedly finds herself in. Usually, we think of grace or benediction as a gift of comfort, security, or pleasure. However, grace usually shows up as a great challenge that lends meaning to life.

The old, weak self is not prepared for the mighty, meaningful challenge. It feels like caving in and copping out. *Why must I needlessly meddle with trouble?* it says. The pull to retreat is strong, and the pressure and inclination to let go of this opportunity are overwhelming.

Nevertheless, hold on.

## The Battle Worth Fighting

Temptations will call. Old habits will return. Familiar voices will tell you to quit. Don't listen, stand still and strong. Don't give up. It's a battle worth fighting. Don't care too much about the result, just don't quit.

And if you can stand through this one, then in all the forthcoming battles of life, victory is guaranteed. Choosing the right battle and standing firm till the very end: isn't that what victory truly is?

# 52 | A Work Worth Your Life

> *Live for something you can die for. Let that be your career."*

Is profession just a way to earn, or is it something much deeper, something that defines your very life?

To ask *which profession to choose* is really to ask: *What is worth doing with this one life?*

Have you ever paused to see how much of your waking time will be spent working? About 70%. That makes this one of the most critical questions of your life: *What is worth doing with this time?*

Work is life, because it consumes so much of your life. If you value yourself, if you care for your one chance at living, wouldn't you want to find out what deserves your devotion?

Look around. Most people stumble into their professions for all the wrong reasons. Someone chases security and ends up in a dull job. Another inherits a business and walks into it without question. No wonder so many are bored, bitter, or chronically irritated.

The quality of your profession is defined not by your income or reputation, but by your inner state. Not by numbers, not by applause, but by the love and energy you bring to it.

## A Work Worth Your Life

Want to know if you're in the right profession? Ask yourself: *Would I still do this if it paid me nothing?* If the answer is yes—if something calls to you so deeply that you'd give your life to it—you've found your work.

And only then is life truly worth living.

# 53 | Immersed or Lost?

> "When you are immersed
> in something worthwhile,
> then trivia and trash find no space within.
> They try to knock but nobody answers,
> so they stay out."

Immersion is powerful. When you're deeply engaged in something meaningful, the petty and the pointless simply don't get through. They may still hover around, trying to distract you, but they find no opening. You are too full of something real.

But beware. Not all immersion is good. The wrong kind of immersion is like anaesthesia. You stop worrying, not because you've resolved anything, but because you've gone unconscious. You are busy, yes, but with senseless tasks, shallow goals, mechanical routines. It feels fine only because your awareness is dulled. Pain fades, but so does clarity. You are not healed. You are only sedated.

That kind of work feels good, but it isn't good. It numbs you. It disconnects you from yourself.

The right kind of immersion is the opposite. It does not dull your senses, it sharpens them. It does not put you to sleep, it wakes you up. It lifts your awareness. It makes you more conscious, more alive.

## Immersed or Lost?

And here is the paradox: immersion in meaningful action makes you more aware, and more open to pain. You feel more. You see more. But you also rise above the pain. You are no longer trapped in the pain-pleasure cycle. You touch something deeper, something beyond reaction.

If you are immersed in the right thing, there is no greater gift. It is transformative. It is liberating.

But immersion in the wrong thing is not engagement. It is being lost.

# 54 | Not Passion. Not Pressure. Just Love.

> *True fulfillment comes not from passion or pressure, but from a deep understanding of what must be done: driven by love, not desire."*

We often say it's great to choose a career based on one's passion. However, passion is as much an external force as peer pressure. One person picks his work bowing to the market, to family expectations, to the usual demands. Another declares: *I'm following my passion!* — as if that were something sacred. But these two are not fundamentally different. If one is better, it's only by a thin margin.

Then there is a decision that arises from the center of clear seeing. You recognize what is truly valuable. You see what is life-affirmative and what is missing. You sense there is something that must be created, protected, shared.

And you do it not because it excites you, not because it promises profit or applause, but because it is inevitable. It is a call that leaves you no escape. A sacred compulsion. A must.

You don't weigh it on scales of attraction or reward. You don't negotiate. You don't postpone. You don't decorate it with romantic slogans. You choose it because it is right. Because it calls you. Because it won't let you sleep.

## Not Passion. Not Pressure. Just Love.

It's not a career move. It's a sacred obligation. You don't do it for joy, you do it out of love. You simply do it, because not doing it would be a betrayal of your own being.

Only then is your work truly appropriate. Only then does it redeem you.

# 55 | Entrepreneurship as a Sacred Calling

> *Shouldn't you ask:*
> *What is life, and what makes*
> *it worth living? Or is entrepreneurship*
> *just about making bigger numbers*
> *than salaried ones do?"*

So you want to start out. Fine. But be clear, and brutally honest: What is it you are really after, and why?

If you are starting something merely to inflate your image, to chase valuations, to outshine your mates, then let's be clear: your venture is not a contribution. It is a curse. A curse upon yourself and the world you inhabit, and would be pretending to serve, at least in front of the roving cameras if your startup does well.

But if there is a larger purpose, if there is a fire in your heart to fix what is broken, to serve what is sacred, to participate in healing this wounded earth, then it makes sense to begin.

This age needs entrepreneurs. But not merely able ones. We need wise entrepreneurs. Wisdom first. Ability can come later. If there is wisdom, ability can be cultivated. But if there is no wisdom, all your skill is just a weapon in the hands of ignorance.

Look around. The world is fractured, exhausted, suffocating under the weight of reckless ambition. If entrepreneurship means anything, it must mean mission. A calling, not a career move. Not a shortcut to early retirement. Not a scheme to fatten your belly and decorate your weekends with indulgence.

Entrepreneurship must be a love affair. A lifelong love affair. Something you would persist in even if it brought no profits, no applause, no easy comforts. Something you would do even if it brought only struggle.

Because only then will you stay the course. Only then will you not sell out. Only then will you not betray yourself.

Entrepreneurship must not be a way to bejewel a hollow life. It must be a way to discover meaning in life.

# 56 | Sacred Selfishness

> *All progress belongs only to those who can stand firm for what is right, even when their own being rebels against them."*

The internal mess we carry is no small thing. It is ancient. We were born with it. It sits in our cells, older than our thoughts, deeper than our upbringing. Fear, greed, jealousy, attachment: these are not just our personal failings. They are the dark inheritance of evolution itself. Every creature carries them.

When we decide to rise, to challenge these ancient forces, we must not expect a picnic. We are declaring war.

The self does not want to grow. It whispers: *Yes, let growth happen: externally. Let us have more money, more status, more comforts. But internally? Let us remain exactly as we are: afraid, insecure, small.*

This is the manifesto of the ego.

But real growth is internal. And internal growth is rarely comfortable. It demands stress, not the confusion of mindless struggle, but the fire of conscious effort.

This is what the ancients called *tapasya*. From the Sanskrit root *tap*: to burn. We step into the flames willingly, so all that is false in us can be incinerated.

And obviously, our old patterns will revolt. Our conditioning will howl. There will be conflict, exhaustion, doubt. And we must endure it. We must not run.

Because inner growth is not one of the things to be taken care of. It is the only thing to be taken care of. When this is settled, everything else begins to fall into place, sometimes with a grace we did not expect.

Ultimately, we are ourselves. And all that we strive for is our own welfare. What could be more important?

It may sound selfish to say so. But only to one who has never enquired into the self. Look closely, and we will see: pure selfishness is not a defect. It is sacred. It is the beginning of all true transformation.

# 57 | A Huge Kitchen Called Life

> *The small things!*
> *How they eat up the bigness of life.*
> *Like a speck of dust in the eye that*
> *shuts out the mighty Sun."*

Cooking, cooking, cooking. Cleaning, cleaning, cleaning. Washing, washing, washing. Is this really what you were born for?

Three kids. One needs footwear, one needs underwear, the husband needs thermal wear. Is this the grand purpose of your existence?

Footwear for the younger one, underwear for the elder, sweaters for the man of the house. Is this your destiny?

If you spend half your life just cooking food, I fail to see the point. What else is hell but a giant kitchen where everyone is forever chopping, stirring, feeding?

A place where each one is reduced to a stomach, and everything exists to be consumed.

I am not deprecating food. Yes, we all must eat. But you are not here merely to cook and eat.

Life is an opportunity to learn, to challenge yourself, to leave the old self behind, to grow into beauty.

Why waste this sacred chance scrubbing utensils?

Isn't there an entire world to explore? An ocean of literature to dive into? Mental and physical barriers to break? Worthy battles to fight?

When will all that happen if the kitchen remains the center of your life?

Time is life. If you love liberation, you will love time. Because time is your only currency toward freedom.

# 58 | The Jungle in a Necktie

> *Is education about making a living, or about having a life worth living?"*

In one crucial respect, animals have done better than human beings. Animals are not burdened with self-consciousness. Their lives are simple, direct, and innocent. They neither aspire to transcendence nor descend into deliberate self-destruction.

Man too is born an animal, but with a dangerous gift: the potential to rise above instinct, or to fall far below it. This potential is not a guarantee. It is a possibility. It must be cultivated. But man, instead of growing it, misuses it.

He builds cities without soul, systems without compassion, institutions without wisdom. And when they are not built on spiritual foundations, they deserve to collapse. If your homes, your careers, your governments do not honour inner truth, they are just elaborate jungles. Better the real jungle, at least nature there is honest.

When did this fall begin?

It began the day we sidelined self-education. When we decided that clarity, awareness, and inner purpose were optional, at best a soft elective.

What was once meant to teach liberation now teaches competition. What was once meant to awaken consciousness now trains ambition. In that quiet shift, education lost its soul.

Real education must ask not just how to earn a living, but how to live rightly.

Not how to succeed outwardly, but how to awaken inwardly.

Not how to accumulate, but how to understand.

Not how to win, but how to be free.

# 59 | The Burden of False Duties

> *If duty feels heavy,*
> *it was never truly yours.*
> *Authentic responsibility uplifts.*
> *Fake responsibility enslaves."*

Most of the time, what people call their 'responsibility' is simply something they've been taught. Ask them: *How do you know this is your responsibility?* and they won't have an answer.

*I must be successful, it's my responsibility to myself.*

*I must have a great career.*

*I must own a house.*

*I must raise my kids a certain way.*

But how do you know you *must* do all this? Where does this 'must' come from?

If our responsibilities were truly ours, fulfilling them would bring joy. The very fact that they feel like a burden proves they are not real.

Real responsibility is a delight. It doesn't weigh you down, it uplifts. And it arises only from self-knowledge. If I know who I am, I'll also know what I must do. That alone is true responsibility. Without self-knowledge, there can be no true responsibility.

## The Burden of False Duties

Yet people appear to act very responsibly, even without a trace of self-knowledge. How is that possible?

Borrowed responsibilities, harrowed life?

# RELATIONSHIPS: THE GREAT ILLUSION

# 60 | Loneliness Is the First Teacher

> *Loneliness has to be understood, not fought or suppressed. Maybe lack of understanding itself is loneliness."*

We don't become lonely, we are born lonely. The seed of separation is already planted at birth. The newborn isn't just adjusting to the outer world, it's already carrying the blueprint of inner loneliness. That's why even an infant cannot bear to be left alone. It longs to be touched, held, seen. And if that doesn't happen, it begins to weep: not out of hunger, not out of pain, but simply because it cannot bear its solitary condition. And the moment the mother appears, the child quietens. All it needed was presence: company, connection, belonging.

This doesn't stop with childhood. It becomes our way of living. The ego, the basic 'I-sense' we are born with, is lonely by definition. It needs something to hold on to. A person. A belief. A label. It says, "I am," but never stops there. It needs to complete the sentence.

*I am a man.*

*I am a professional.*

*I am a devotee.*

*I am a victim.*

*I am in love.*

The 'I' is never content on its own. It keeps adding objects to itself, hoping that the next one will finally bring peace.

But it never works. It cannot. Because the ego can survive only in incompleteness.

Loneliness is this incompleteness: the restless expectation that something out there will plug the inner gap. And unless you understand this tendency, you will remain lonely. You may keep changing companions, religions, jobs, identities. But the hunger will persist. The I will keep searching for something new to attach itself to.

And if this deep hunger is not understood, it doesn't disappear, it merely goes underground. Suppressed loneliness turns toxic. People run from it into noise, distractions, shallow relationships, addictions, even positive-looking pursuits. But the running only makes it worse. Suppressed pain does not heal, it festers.

But if you're honest enough to stay with your loneliness, something beautiful begins to unfold. When you stop fighting it and start observing it, loneliness becomes a teacher. Creativity, depth, and truth begin to emerge.

The songs that stir us the deepest aren't born in celebration, they rise from quiet heartbreak. The art that survives is not painted in moments of distraction, but drawn from the deepest silence of longing and loss.

Happy moments may bring excitement, but it is suffering that brings sincerity. One who has never suffered cannot write a real song. One who has never wept cannot sing. All art, all wisdom, all courage arise from the willingness to sit with inner turmoil, not to suppress it.

To be free of loneliness, you must walk into it. Understand it. Let it speak. And it will slowly reveal not just its face, but also yours.

# 61 | Loneliness Is the Crowd Within

> *The lonely fellow is the one who is not alright with being alone."*

To be lonely is not the same as being physically alone. It is to be internally crowded: surrounded not by people, but by your own thoughts, comparisons, desires, and memories. Loneliness is not the absence of others, but the obsessive presence of oneself.

The lonely person is constantly thinking about what he lacks, what he deserves, what others have, and why life isn't giving him what he wants. His mind is packed. Cluttered with himself. He may be in a room full of people, yet entirely trapped in personal concerns.

Loneliness is not an empty dinner table, it's a restaurant packed to the brim, but serving stale and distasteful dishes. You sit at a coffee table meant for two. On one chair sit your fantasies. On the other, your fears. And these two parts of you sit locked in a tired, self-pitying conversation. You cannot hear the world. You cannot see the sky. You cannot taste the coffee. Because you're too busy being with yourself.

There's an entire universe around you, vibrant and inviting. But you remain cut off from it, because you demand that it first conform to your expectations. Unless the world behaves the way you want, you won't open up to it. So, instead of embracing what is, you keep clinging to your inner movie. And the movie isn't even pleasant. You don't even enjoy your own company. That's why loneliness hurts.

The lonely one is not with the world and not truly with himself either. He lives in a middle zone of dissatisfaction: isolated from life, addicted to mind.

Being alone, however, is something entirely different. To be alone is to be whole. To be alone is to have no holes that need plugging. Aloneness is not about exclusion, it's about inner sufficiency. In aloneness, you relate to the world as a healthy one, not to suck out of it, but simply to meet it.

# 62 | Purpose First, Person Later

> *"That's the only love worth having: a fierce, uncompromising love for greatness. Not someone else's greatness, but your own."*

Especially today, you don't need a man or a woman to survive or feel secure. The economy feeds you. Systems protect you. Hospitals heal you. Apps deliver your groceries. You can earn. You can live. You can manage.

So stop pretending that a person is your primary need. They are not. Your real need is something far more sacred. Find that. Serve that. Live for that.

If you don't fill your life with clarity, depth, and beauty, you will be condemned to stuff it with garbage. And often, that garbage takes the shape of a person. A warm body. A familiar voice. A comforting lie.

Don't let that happen to you. Don't turn your life into a landfill of emotional scraps. Don't decorate your hollowness with company.

Rise. Refine. Reclaim your inner throne. See what kind of love silently reveals itself to you.

# 63 | Valuable or Merely Vulnerable?

> *The presence of insecurity in a relationship doesn't say anything about its value or worth. It only shows a lack of health.*

Insecurity in relationships is evident when you want to clutch and hold things tightly. Insecurity arises when desire is the foundation of the relationship. Desire, by its nature, is insecure.

So, are you relating with the other for your personal gain, prestige, or pleasure? Then does the relationship have any real substance? And if it lacks substance, what exactly are you trying to secure?

If something is truly valuable, then it has strength. What else is ever valuable in a relationship?

Look at the dissonance: On one hand, we say the relationship is valuable. On the other, we call it fragile and vulnerable. These two don't go together.

If it is valuable, it cannot be so vulnerable. And if it is vulnerable—prone to influences, to conditions, to the changing weather, to mood swings—then what value does it really have?

# 64 | Hurt Is When Fantasy Breaks

*Attachment and hurt are one and the same. One is seen in the beginning, the other in the end."*

If you are hurt, investigate your attachment.

Hurt is not random. It is the collapse of a story you were secretly clinging to. A picture shattered, a belief jolted, an expectation denied.

Can there be hurt without ownership? Without desire? You hurt most where you want most, where your identity is invested.

Strangers rarely hurt you. It is those you try to possess, define, and control. When they defy your image of them, pain arises.

Hurt is reality exposing illusion. You imagined something. Reality said otherwise.

It is born of craving, assumption, and sleep. You wanted, you believed, you expected. Reality refused. So you suffered.

Truth cannot be hurt. Only the ego breaks. Only the dreamer bleeds.

To live without illusions is to be free of hurt. Not because pain stops, but because the false self no longer stands to lose.

Hurt is not your enemy. It is the alarm bell of attachment. Hear it, and wake up.

# 65 | Desire Invests, Love Nurtures

> *If the other exists in your life to serve your needs, there can be no love. There would be a lot of attachment, dependency, clutching, suffering! Relate to give, or relate for a purposeless joy."*

As long as a relationship is based on need, it will remain a relationship of violence. For most of us, love is just another form of desire. And desire always invests to get returns. So our love becomes an investment, expecting payback. The greater your love appears, the greater your urge to recover your investment in the other. What else is violence?

I invest in someone only to get returns. When those returns don't come, I go breathless, I panic, I stamp my feet, I pull the other's hair, I pull out my own hair. And mostly, I don't even have the courage to acknowledge this orgy of frustration.

Where does this frustration come from? It comes from confusing love with desire. Desire invests, love nurtures. A person without self-knowledge will live constantly in desire, and will remain incapable of love.

# 66 | Half and Half Is a Quarter

> *The best relationships are not born out of loneliness. Loneliness breeds dependence and exploitation in relationships."*

Most relationships begin not from fullness, but from lack. People come together because they need each other.

*I need you, and you need me.*

*I'll fulfill your desire, and you'll fulfill mine.*

It's a connection born not of love, but of mutual utility.

And the day someone becomes useless—when they no longer serve your emotional, physical, or social needs—it suddenly feels unnecessary, even difficult, to continue with them. The bond weakens. Affection fades. Because it was never love. It was a transaction.

Relationships can be beautiful: nourishing, expansive, even sacred. But only if we do not inject them with selfishness. Only if the other is not reduced to a tool for our gratification.

If the other exists in your life only to serve your needs, there can be no love. There may be attachment, dependency, obsession, but not love.

Relate—relate prolifically—but from a place of inner richness. Relate without the hollow. Don't use the other to plug your emptiness. Don't turn them into a bandage for your wounds.

That is not love. That is fear wearing the mask of intimacy. That is loneliness disguised as connection.

Let your relationships arise from clarity, not craving. Let them be expressions of joy, not escapes from pain.

Only then do they become real. Only then do they become free.

# 67 | When Closeness Becomes a Cage

> *The true lover wants you free, the false lover wants you dependent."*

A relationship of dependence cannot be a healthy relationship. A relationship in which the other becomes central to your well-being is not a welcome situation.

Even when everything seems to be going well in a relationship, keep checking: Have I become dependent? Have I turned exploitative? Have I started holding self-centred expectations? Has the other started expecting too much? Has the other come so close that he is blocking my view of the larger universe? Has the other become too central in my mind and thoughts? Has the other started occupying my inner space to an extent that may be called unhealthy?

These are the things you should watch for when there are no troubling symptoms. Often, when the symptoms appear, it is already too late.

# 68 | Love That Sets You Free

> *If you want to test a relationship, if you want to test the quality of your company, start talking real stuff with them, or just start blocking the nonsense.*

Do you think you are in love with a person?

Please check what the company of that person brings to you. Does it make you turbulent, or does it make you peaceful?

Does the person want to make himself felt, or does he empower you to be independently secure?

Has insecurity and possessiveness been aroused in you, or have you rather turned more mature and secure in his company?

A real lover will empower you. He will bring you closer to your assured self.

He will say, *You are complete even if I am not with you. Not that I want to be away, but even if I am away you are still complete.* The fake lover will say, *Without me your life is incomplete, so you better cling to me.*

A true lover will have a stake in your well-being. A false lover will have a stake in your dependencies. He will want you to remain dependent—emotionally, physically, financially—in some way or the other.

The true lover will want you to be totally free of everything, including himself.

# 69 | Mr Hormones Again!

> *Common love is not the poetic longing you think it is. It's a hormonal explosion masquerading as romance. Love is lost the moment you mistake chemistry for divinity."*

Have you ever seen anyone walk up honestly and say: *You know what, my hormones get wildly activated when I see you?* Nobody says that. They don't even realise it.

Instead, they declare: *Darling, I have fallen in love.*

Have you ever seen a six-year-old falling madly in love? Why does this "love" always erupt at sixteen?

Don't you see, it's not love. It's raw chemistry. One chemical cocktail trying to mix with another. Male-chemical, female-chemical, and then: explosion.

It is as ridiculous as it sounds. But you refuse to leave it at that. You make it grave. You write songs, weep tears, call it heartbreak, call it destiny.

Next time someone proposes "love," try replying: *Ho ho ho, Mr. Hormones!*

## Mr Hormones Again!

And remember: hormones rarely introduce themselves as hormones. They often dress up as sincerity, as longing, as genuine connection.

But peel the mask, and it's the same old biological urge, just better disguised.

Most of what the world calls genuine love is biochemical frenzy hiding behind emotional urges and soulful utterances.

# 70 | I Love You, Seriously?

> *The moment your needs are not fulfilled, what you called love turns into frustration and blame."*

There exists an unfortunate couple.

She doesn't directly say, *Get me a dress.* When she wants a dress, she says, *Darling, you don't love me.* And he understands: she needs a dress.

He too doesn't need to say he wants sex. All he has to say is, *I love you.* And she understands what he means. When he says, *I love you,* he means: undress.

A miserable couple, indeed. Wish there were none like them.

As a man or a woman, you may think the fulfilment of your desires is the culmination of love, but that is self-deception. Exchange of pleasure, barter of goods and services: this is not love.

Is love about gratification of the self, or dissolution of the self?

Please meditate on this.

# 71 | Love That Breaks under Heat

> "Love that is chemical is just a reaction. Love is possible only when the lover has a deep devotion to something beyond chemistry."

If you look carefully, what happens between any two human beings is so much a game of circumstances. A play of chemicals, randomness: all so conditional. A little heat, some spatial intimacy, some catalyst, and almost any chemical can combine with any other. Suitable conditions can make anybody relate with anybody.

A hydrogen molecule relates with an oxygen molecule. There is a certain bonding, a certain transformation when the two come together. Superficially, it appears that both have surrendered their individuality, and something new has resulted from their union. But those who know chemicals know better. The two combined under certain situations, and another set of situations would tear them apart.

One is tricked into believing that both hydrogen and oxygen have disappeared. They aren't gone. They are just hiding. The molecule can split any day, any moment. The conditions will change, the molecule will split, and you will find that oxygen and hydrogen have reappeared. They were never really gone; they were only hidden.

That is our normal human love: as objects meet objects. Such unions exist only under certain conditions. When the conditions change, the dream is over.

Can there be love beyond chemistry? Does the self want to ingratiate itself, or dissolve itself? Dissolution can come only when the self sees itself as needless. This seeing is at the core of all wisdom. It is self-awareness, the *sine qua non* for love.

# 72 | Love beyond Fantasy

> *Love is not about possessing someone; it is about liberating yourself from the need to possess."*

When all your hopes are dashed, when you finally see that love is simply impossible between unconscious human beings, only then does real love become possible.

To realise that ordinary love is not love at all is the beginning of awakening. You see you have been chasing the impossible for too long. Real love begins when you drop these hollow hopes.

False hope always ends in hurt. And love is the greatest healer because it prevents you from getting hurt in the first place. We keep imagining that somewhere, someday, some magical person will fill the emptiness in our heart. We keep expecting, until the inevitable disappointment comes. Complete freedom from that expectation is the birth of real love.

Bring clarity into your life. See your bondages, and dismantle them. Drop the incompletion by understanding how your instincts and desires arise and operate.

Then love will not remain a distant fantasy. It will be your natural state.

# 73 | Echoes of Emptiness

> *Being incomplete, you are seeking completeness from another incomplete one. Isn't it the case of two beggars uniting in the hope that the union will produce a billionaire? It does not."*

If you believe a man or woman will bring peace to your mind or godliness to your home, you're inviting deep disappointment.

Ah, the disillusioned couples! She imagined he would add spine to her dull life, be her anchor, her strength. But the man is spineless, not just bodily, but spiritually. Soon, she wonders: *I thought he would be a pillar of support. I don't know what kind of flaccid pillar he is, never upright enough to support anything!*

Then begins the familiar drama, what the world calls marriage. He wants an omelette; she has no eggs. She wants to talk; he wants silence. She seeks depth; he seeks distraction.

Neither has what the other truly needs. They came incomplete, seeking completion. Hollow within, they echo each other's emptiness.

This is what happens when you expect salvation from the other. But the other is just as lost.

## Echoes of Emptiness

No one can bring light to your home unless it already burns within you. No partner can offer peace unless you've begun walking the inner path.

Without that, it's not love. It's a quiet trade in confusion, a drama of disappointment.

# 74 | Love You as You Are?

*Being with no one is far, far better than being with the wrong one."*

Is your lover empowering you, or enfeebling you? Are they liberating you or slowly enslaving you in the name of care? Someone who limits you, who cages you—always under the pretense of care—is no friend and certainly no lover.

Someone who lets you rot comfortably in your weaknesses is no gift to your life. Someone who never dares to tear down your falseness is only reinforcing your prison. Someone who sighs, *I love you exactly as you are,* is your deadliest sedative.

Run.

Your lover must be someone who refuses you, again and again, forty times a day if needed. Someone who won't collude with your illusions. Someone who wounds your ego so your truth can breathe. Not out of cruelty, but out of deep compassion for what you can become.

Love is fire. It burns away what you are not. How can you stay with someone who whispers: *Stay small. Stay dull. Stay mine?* Don't even wait for the cab, bolt for your life.

# 75 | Romancing Infinity

> *Infinity is neither imagination nor something beyond it. Infinity lies in relentlessly challenging your finite limits."*

At any level, the maximum you can do is enough. You're not asked to go beyond your capacity, but you are absolutely required to reach its edge.

That's the challenge: Not to exceed your capacity, but to exhaust it.

Once you do that, once you truly give your all, you begin to see results. And once results arrive, discipline becomes easier. Now you've tasted the formula: *The more I exert, the more I receive.* You've seen the proof. Now you're convinced. Now you're dangerous. Now you're unstoppable.

But here's the trick: At your current level, you must do at least enough to generate some result. Even a small one. Because if you don't, you'll be left with nothing: no reward, no motivation.

And that's the worst place to be: You've worked. You've suffered. But not enough to move the needle. So your scorecard reads zero. No gain. No momentum. No faith.

You're tired, but unrewarded. You've paid the price, but bought nothing.

So remember: Infinity never demands the impossible. It only demands that you hold nothing back.

# 76 | Tried Attachment? Now Try Love

> *"You stay in a room long enough, you may get attached to the room. You use a shirt or car for a period of time, and again there is identification. Keep copper and zinc in contact long enough, and they start fusing into each other. You want to call this love?"*

Attachment feels pleasant, doesn't it? However, can we calmly examine attachment and see that it obviously comes with violence, fear, greed, delusion, boredom, loneliness, suspicion, and the rest of it?

Attachment feels like love. But isn't attachment always self-centred? Attachment cannot be love.

Much of the hell that we endure in the name of love does not actually come from love at all. From fear to loneliness, all the afflictions arrive in a bunch with attachment. Attachment feels good. What comes with attachment feels unbearable.

To quit all that which comes along with attachment, there is no option but to see the dangerous hollowness of attachment. Then the only route left is that of love.

## Tried Attachment? Now Try Love

One tries so much in the name of love. Only love remains untried. Good idea to give love a chance? Nah. Love is not an idea.

# 77 | You Become What You Love

> *If you love the mud, you will become an earthworm. If you love the Sky, you will grow wings.*"

False love is a slippery slope. You don't have to do anything to slide down, you just fall. That's why they say, "fall in love." It takes no effort to descend.

But true love is different. True love is a climb. It demands conscious determination. It won't possess you unless you allow it. It won't dominate you unless you bow to it.

And that's the tragedy: Even the Highest needs your permission to enter. And that permission rarely comes.

Love won't just happen. You have to choose it. You have to surrender to it. In the tug-of-war between convenience and love, the right choice won't make itself. You have to make it.

Love is a choice. And the temptation to side with comfort is always there. But remember: If you keep choosing the mud, don't be surprised when you forget how to fly.

# 78 | Love Happens Outside the Script

> *Love is not natural.*
> *What comes naturally to humans*
> *is jungle love: territorial, hormonal, possessive.*
> *Real love begins only when jungle love is*
> *transcended, and social*
> *love is unlearned."*

The more clearly you see how deeply conditioned you are, the less shocked you'll be by how conditioned others are. We are not individuals, we are scripts. Trained, programmed, predictable.

But because we don't see our own conditioning, life keeps surprising us. We keep asking: *How could he do that? How could she change so suddenly?*

But when you're in touch with reality, nothing surprises you. Scripts behave like scripts. That's all. You thought you were dating a woman. She's not a woman, she's a script. She thought she was dating a man. You're not a man, you're a script.

It's not a relationship. It's a collision of patterns. And as long as the script is running, there is no space for love. The possibility of love opens up only when the script is paused, questioned, dismantled.

# 79 | Their Longing Is Yours

> *If you can remember the fact of your own bondage and your desire for your own freedom, then you become intensely sensitive to the fact of other's bondage, and to their unspoken longing for freedom.*

When you truly love yourself, you realize something startling: your welfare and the welfare of the world are inseparable.

Ordinary love is just the urge to barter comforts, to trade pleasures, to seduce or be seduced. Real love is something altogether different. It is the clear recognition that the other is exactly like you.

And who are you? You are the restless one, the suffering one. You are the one who carries a gnawing incompleteness. Loving yourself means giving yourself that which alone can end this hunger: truth, not consolation; liberation, not distraction.

Love yourself enough to refuse the mediocre, the lowly, the momentary. Demand the Highest for yourself.

And the other is no different. The other too aches to fill the hollow in the heart. The other too is tired of the lifelong ache. This shared recognition, this knowledge that we are companions in the same crisis, is love.

## Their Longing Is Yours

Let your love for the Highest shape how you meet others. Assist them exactly as you assist yourself. Serve them not out of pity or duty, but out of a deep remembrance that their story is your story, and their longing is your own.

# 80 | Be Whole before You Belong

> *Before you can become a worthy partner, isn't it necessary to become a worthy person?"*

You must learn aloneness. Before you relate with people, you must be very, very comfortable with yourself. If you are someone who cannot be with herself comfortably, easily, gladly, then kindly spare the other person. If you are not alright with yourself, don't start piggybacking on the other. And usually it is that way; you go to the other precisely because you are not okay with yourself.

At the same time, we must remember that we will have to relate with each other. We are not going to live insulated or isolated; we are going to be related. But the relationship has to be healthy. You should not become a burden on the other. You should not carry your pathology to the other.

Read. Learn to travel alone. Watch movies alone. Play. There is so much that can be done only in your aloneness. And that will make you very strong from within, fulfilled, complete in yourself. Then you will not approach the other as a beggar.

Then, even if you approach the other, even if you relate, it will be a relationship of health, a relationship in which you have something to give. A relationship of joy, not of dependence and desperation.

# 81 | Real Love Is Never Incidental

> *A conditioned self can never know love. I'll love you forever is often just a poetic way of saying: Until you stop pleasing me."*

What is usually called love is just a bundle of conditions, and it survives only as long as those conditions remain favourable. It stings to hear this, doesn't it?

For centuries, wide-eyed couples—enchanted by each other's voice, brawn, colour, or curves—have stood under the stars, hand on heart, swearing: *I'll love you till eternity.* And then lived long enough to confess how hollow that vow really was.

This is conditional love. Love that exists only as long as the weather is kind, the mood is sweet, the benefits mutual. The moment those conditions disappear, even the illusion of love begins to crumble.

Unconditional love becomes possible only when you see the futility of getting attached to fleeting things. When you gather the courage to admit: chasing bubbles is amusing for a while, but you cannot build a life on soap and air.

## Real Love Is Never Incidental

Only when you reject the accidental, the random and the circumstantial do you come upon something real. Only then does love stop being a transaction and become a revelation.

Freedom from the incidental is the beginning of real love.

Not attraction. Not attachment. Love.

# 82 | Watch the Effect, Not the Person

> *How does one get into the right relationship? Not by searching for the right person. Involve yourself in a worthy project, and then the one who helps you accomplish that project is worthy of being related to.*

Right companionship is a blessing. Never prevent yourself from being with a person, or many persons, if they illumine your mind and uplift your life.

What is marriage? Firstly, it is an arrangement of companionship. You are committing yourself to be with someone, possibly for many decades. So more than anything else, the question of marriage should be about the quality of the impact your partner has upon your mind.

If someone's presence has a becalming and liberating effect on your mind, go ahead, boldly be with that person as much as you want. On the other hand, how do you benefit from the greatest meal in the world if your system is allergic to it?

Remember, it is not the partner that counts, but the effect that the partner's company has on your life. We get so lost in watching our partner that we forget to watch our own condition. What makes a person great is not his intellect, fame, wealth, or body. What makes him great is the greatness you achieve in his company.

# 83 | Blind Union, Lifelong Prison

> *As wise men and women, if you are married, wonderful. As wise men and women, if you are not married, wonderful. The point is not really the marriage. The point is wisdom.*"

I have nothing for or against marriage. What matters to me is the mind of man, the mind that rushes toward security, that wants to possess and hold captive another human being. That's the mind I wish to examine.

Marriage often shapes the kind of work you do. It affects your relationship with the children you bring into the world. It influences nearly every aspect of your life. That's why I speak of marriage: not to prescribe it, but to prompt self-inquiry.

My work is not to hand you instructions. It is to help you look within. And what you find inside is far more important than any social arrangement. Your relationship with yourself is deeper than your relationship with another.

Two people can live together for life, and it can be beautiful. But what if they came together in blindness? What if they didn't know what they were doing? What if they had no understanding of self, body, love, desire, or exploitation?

What if the mistake is final, stamped with the permanence of ignorance?

# 84 | Loving the Person or the Ghost?

> *We don't love people, we love the ghosts of our own imagination, until reality bursts the bubble."*

We don't love people. We love the ghosts of our own imagination, until reality shatters the dream.

Don't you see how experience fools you every single day? Look at your girlfriend: there she stands, and you swear she's the most beautiful woman in the world. That's the sheer delusional power of your perception.

We live steeped in self-deception. Even when we think we are looking at ordinary people, we are really staring at projections. Ghosts. Hallucinations in broad daylight.

Classically, this is called living not in Truth. Not in fact, but in phenomenon: hollow sensory appearances, mental mirages.

What is a ghost? That which does not exist, yet seems to.

So, even your beloved is a ghost, because the one you claim to love isn't who they truly are. It is an image you have carefully assembled, one that flatters your ego, calms your fears, and props up your insecurities. You worship the image. You avoid the real person.

## Loving the Person or the Ghost?

But illusion cannot hide forever. The day you grow intimate and meet the actual person behind the fantasy, friction begins. Disillusionment follows. The bubble bursts, and it hurts.

Try not to live inside bubbles. They explode. And that hurts.

# 85 | Beyond Forgiveness

> *You hold grudges because you expect others to fit your images; they don't, and your desires feel wounded. Real forgiveness is when you drop those expectations so fully that there is nothing left to forgive.*

You expected people to behave in a certain way, and they didn't. And your expectations empowered them over you while leaving you vulnerable. Relieve others of your expectations. The other is who they are, not the image you hold of them.

It is only your desirous expectations that feel hurt when people don't match them. To see that most people are conditioned machines, bound to behave in predictable ways, that is forgiveness.

Forgiveness is not just suppressing the urge to take revenge. Real forgiveness is not needing to forgive at all. As long as you feel the need to forgive, you are still clinging to petty things in the mind: hurts, distortions, complaints.

Only if you still feel offended does the question of forgiving arise: *Should I forgive? But he gave me such a nasty blow!*

Real forgiveness is when you have moved past those little things and have simply forgotten the hurt. Letting go becomes easier when there is something truly important to take care of.

# THOUGHT, BELIEF, AND THE TRAP OF KNOWLEDGE

# 86 | The Stainless Mind

> *"To be unreactive is to have the lively capacity to respond consciously, not impulsively. It is to engage with all situations without letting the situations distort the one engaging."*

We need a mind that does not leap into reaction. A mind that acts—beautifully, fiercely—but never compulsively or unconsciously. One that moves not out of provocation, but out of clarity.

The more reactive you are, the more your actions become borrowed. They stop being yours. They become helpless echoes of what someone else did. There is no agency in that. No originality. Just a loop of wounds reacting to wounds.

Consider your cooking vessels. You prepare something in oil and spice, and residue clings to the inner surface. In everyday language, the vessel is stained. In the language of chemistry, a bond has formed.

That which we call a bond in daily life, we call bondage in spirituality. Why do bonds even form? Because atoms are not perfectly stable. They feel incomplete. They carry excess energy. So they reach out—donating, accepting, or sharing electrons—in search of rest.

## The Stainless Mind

The human mind is no different. It is chemical, unstable, restless. It keeps looking around to form associations, to cling, to settle down into something. Anything. That is what makes it so eager to react.

But just as you dislike it when your vessels get sticky, you must learn not to like it when your mind clings. Eventually, you buy better cookware. Stainless, non-stick. Not because the ingredients have changed. You still cook the same dishes. But now, the pan does not retain residue.

That is how the mind should be. Capable of action, fully involved, yet untouched. It participates in life, yet walks away clean. It performs without being stained.

That is the stainless mind. That is real freedom.

# 87 | Fluency without Insight Is Noise

> *When expression comes from the rush of ignorance and desire, there is fear within, due to the absence of clarity. To offset this fear, one depends on tricks like willpower and confidence."*

In the prevailing culture, there is a strange and excessive emphasis on public speaking. We've elevated confident expression into a benchmark of intelligence, even of personal worth. Confidence, especially when loud and shallow, has become the new ideal.

There's an ad I often come across. A little kid, probably five or eight, is standing on stage, finger pointed at the audience, as if delivering wisdom to the world. His face radiates a kind of rehearsed self-assurance: sharp gestures, glowing confidence, theatrical expression. And this, it seems, is what the culture now aspires to: speak with flair, even if there's no substance. Expressiveness without insight. Volume without depth.

The message is simple: if you speak fluently, you're worth listening to. And if you can confidently spout gibberish, you're celebrated. This is what we now reward.

But expression, or any performance skill, is no indicator of a meaningful life. What matters far more is whether you have something worth expressing. And if you do, then the manner of your expression becomes secondary.

If you had to put it in numbers, ninety-five percent of value lies in the core: what you are actually seeing, living, and saying. Five percent, if at all, belongs to external tools: your accent, vocabulary, fluency, posture, and confidence. And even that five percent is an overestimation.

Where does quality come from? It comes from attentiveness. From sincerity. From an honest relationship with life.

When words come from clarity, willpower is not needed. Clarity itself is an unstoppable force.

But the marketplace thrives on insincerity, because only the distracted can be sold illusions. So it promotes a culture of hollow expressiveness. Talk fast, talk loud, talk endlessly. And if you look good doing it, you'll be rewarded, by others who are just as lost.

Ignorance applauds ignorance, especially when it's dressed in confidence.

*Oh, he's so fluent! I'm impressed!*

You should know better.

Be impressed by the right things. Because what you admire is what you start becoming.

# 88 | You Can't Create Creativity

> *When one is not caught in mundane rubbish, creativity just happens. You don't develop it, you only remove what blocks it. You can't cause creativity, but you can invite it. It comes on its own when it finds a clean space to enter."*

What blocks creativity? A cluttered mind. A mind obsessed, anxious, worried. A mind too dependent on the outcome of its own efforts.

Creativity is uncertain. And so are its results. If you are someone who worries too much about the results, you simply cannot be creative. The need for certainty kills creation.

To create is to bring into being something truly new, something untouched by the past, by conditioning, by the security of known patterns. What we usually call innovation—a new twist, a repurposed idea, a better version—is not creativity. It is refinement, not birth.

Creativity has to be purposeless. All purpose is drawn from memory. Even the noblest purpose is just a polished desire from yesterday. Purpose binds. It brings fear: the fear of failure, of missing out, of not reaching the goal. In a mind dominated by fear, creativity cannot arise.

True creativity requires a mind that is not chasing a result. A mind that is not striving for validation. It requires inner freedom. And inner freedom is not something you achieve by effort, it is what remains when the inner noise falls silent.

# 89 | No Habit Is a Good Habit

> *Life is a constant tug-of-war between habit and choice. And habit almost always wins, because it disguises itself as choice.*

A habit means just two things. First, you keep repeating something. Second, you have no real understanding of why you do it. It happens automatically, like a reflex in a dead body. A button is pressed, a pattern is triggered. No intelligence, no questioning.

When habit takes over, you vanish. There is no you in that moment. Later, you might remember, you might repent, you might promise yourself you won't do it again. But when it is happening, you are absent. You are a puppet dangling on invisible strings.

And yet, look at the irony: people proudly talk of "good habits." As if unconscious repetition can ever be good. For a Jain, not eating meat is called a good habit. For someone else, butchering animals on festivals is the same good habit. Same action, different slogans. Same blindness.

Do you really know why you refuse meat? Do you really know why you crave blood? Or are you just recycling what was stuffed into your head before you could think for yourself? That is habit. Something you do every day, but have never once examined.

## No Habit Is a Good Habit

Can anything unconscious be called good? When you label it a good habit, you are just putting perfume on ignorance. Recognise this without flinching: No habit is a good habit. No habit is harmless.

Habit is the silent killer of intelligence. It makes you dull, mechanical, predictable. When you truly understand something, habit dissolves. When you see clearly, no pattern can control you.

So start paying ruthless attention. Watch yourself in small things and big ones. And ask: *Am I doing this because I am fully alive, or because I am already half-dead?*

# 90 | Stay Uncertain, Stay Alive

> *It's better to be confused while inquiring, experimenting, investigating, than to live in the false confidence that one knows it all."*

You don't need confidence. You need honesty and inquiry. You need inquiry and honesty. It is better to suspend confidence and conclusions than to be falsely confident.

Most people you find radiating confidence might actually be using confidence to mask insecurity or ignorance. So, remain an inquirer. Accept that when things are uncertain and knowledge is incomplete, one can still be alright. Accept that enquiry needs to continue and conclusions should be postponed.

Enquiry is difficult and uncomfortable because the mind wants quick settlements. It resists staying with uncertainty and unpredictability. It wants to quickly certify itself in binary.

The facts of life are otherwise. They demand rigorous inquiry and continuous attention. We idolize those who emphatically say: *I know*. We don't much like those who say: *I'm trying to know*, because our emphasis is on success, on results, and then on consuming the results. We work intending to quickly extract happiness from the results. With such an intent, obviously the process of inquiry does not remain enjoyable.

Joy lies in the inquiry itself. Or does joy lie in concluding, closing or arriving? Is it in an easy, and often false, destination, or in travelling rightly?

It's alright if you don't come across as a very confident person. Remain skeptical of conclusions, keep travelling. If there's no joy in the journey, how can there be joy in life?

# 91 | The Blabber We Call Life

> *"Our entire existence is shaped by hollow concepts fed to us, yet we continue to act as though we truly understand them."*

These words are the foundation of every step we take:

You act because you think you are *responsible*.

You cling because you think it is *love*.

You stay because you think there are *duties* to fulfil.

You crave a *future* you don't understand.

You compromise because you think a *relationship* must be saved.

We base our lives on words like love and responsibility, yet we rarely ask what they truly mean. Every breath is lived atop these borrowed assumptions. And that's not just unfortunate, it's tragic.

Just observe how people converse. Look at them. You'll feel tempted to exclaim: What kind of madhouse is this?

A is babbling nonsense to B, without the faintest idea of what he's saying. B nods solemnly and replies, equally clueless. Neither knows where their thoughts, words, or impulses come from. Yet A speaks with conviction, and B nods with understanding.

## The Blabber We Call Life

This spectacle of mutual ignorance doesn't prevent either from feeling a sweet glow of connection. At the end of it, they'll declare they are in love. A fresh drama begins.

And what kind of children will this unexamined union produce?

It only gets more grotesque from here, so let's spare ourselves the rest of the horror.

# 92 | Why Motivation Fails

> "You don't need motivation. You need realization. You don't need a push. You don't need a pull. You need the source, the one that powers from within. And it's already there. You've simply forgotten the key."

All motivation is external. Someone says a few fiery words, and suddenly you feel a surge. You watch an inspiring film, and you feel charged. You read a story, and you feel moved. But what is really happening here?

An external force is acting upon you. You are reacting. That is not freedom. That is not clarity. That is not even your energy: it is borrowed. And what is borrowed can never last. The speech ends, and the motivation vanishes. The movie ends, and the energy fizzles out. The book closes, and so does your resolve.

Even worse, one force pushes you in one direction, another in the opposite. Your father says one thing, the media says another, your guru says a third. Whom do you obey? You are pulled in ten directions, none of which are truly yours.

This is not a conscious life. This is slavery to impressions. It's confusion dressed as passion.

Real action does not arise from motivation. Real, rooted, vibrant action arises from realization. From understanding. From the quiet power of intelligence.

The external can, at best, take you back to yourself. That's all it can do. And that's enough, because when you touch your inner source, no push is needed.

Real energy is not about hype. It is about seeing. And when you see clearly, you act rightly, without the need to be pushed.

# 93 | Why Self-Help Doesn't Help

> *"What you call 'self-help' is often just the ego's desperate survival strategy. Helping the self is futile. Seeing through it is liberation."*

Most self-help is about helping your ego to protect itself. The ego wants to protect itself from the consequences of its flawed existence and ignorant deeds. Such protection is impossible, but the ego believes that with some help from somewhere, it might pull it off. When a loud demand for help exists, there is bound to be plenty of opportunistic supply as well: that's the concept and industry of self-help.

Shouldn't we ask: what is this 'self' that self-help seeks to help? Who are you, and who am I? And since I do not quite know who I am, maybe that's the reason I am running around with a hundred issues, seeking solace in 'self-help', among other placebos.

Self-help spawns books, seminars, videos, methods, but do they ever tell you what your own nature and reality is? How is it possible to help the self without knowing the self? It may be possible, given the terrible state of the self, that you need not self-help but self-dissolution.

Behind the sophisticated façade and the clever turns of phrase, the raw self-help philosophy basically is: *I am sad because my desires stand unfulfilled. So, fulfilling desires is the way to help the self.*

They won't tell you that fulfilling desires is nowhere the same thing as fulfilling yourself. Therefore, self-help pleases but doesn't help. It is not then 'self-help'; the genre should be correctly called self-gratification.

If you want self-gratification, as we all do, then there are so many means and ways available. People entertain themselves, drink, take to narcotics, go high on money, on power, hunt for carnal pleasures. These are all ways in which we try to 'help' the self by fulfilling its desires. Unfortunately, these ways don't work. Self-help is attractive but not beneficial.

Real self-help lies in understanding the nature of the self, by honest self-observation. And from this observation, goodness follows spontaneously.

# 94 | Freedom from Positivity

> *"When you reject your weaknesses, you no longer need 'positive' thoughts to prop you up. Positivity often conceals fear. True freedom is when positivity becomes redundant."*

For you to call something "positive," there must first be a centre, an origin, a frame of reference. Depending on where that centre is, one thing becomes positive, and another negative.

But our centres are conditioned, personal, and egoic. That's why every person has a different definition of what is positive or negative: because their centres differ. So the words "positive" and "negative" become not just relative, but often misleading and dangerous.

When we call something positive, are we not usually saying that it pleases our ego? The ego rushes toward what it finds agreeable. But ego never walks alone: it always brings duality. Wherever there's positivity, negativity follows. Wherever there is positivity, negativity is not far behind. In chasing the "positive," one unknowingly invites its shadow.

The more the ego craves pleasure, the more it opens itself to pain. What feels positive today may appear hollow, or even harmful, tomorrow. And in this constant swing between what pleases and what displeases, so much of your energy is drained.

Positive and negative both arise from the ego-centre. They are not truths, only fleeting moods of a shifting mind. Why run after what is so fleeting?

You chase positivity only when haunted by negativity. When afraid, anxious, or disturbed, you reach for positive thoughts like a medicine. But what if you were so deeply assured, so anchored, that you didn't need any "positive" reinforcement at all?

The very demand for positivity reveals inner fear. True peace is when you are so seated in something real, something unshakeable, that you don't require external support, not even in the form of a comforting 'positive' thought.

Reject all voices, including the internal one, that say you are incomplete, insecure, or lacking. You do not need any crutches. All supports—people, affirmations, ideas—are themselves weak. They need you more than you need them. Depending on anything outside for your peace will only prolong your unrest.

From inner ignorance arises the demand for positivity. Freedom from dependency is freedom from positivity.

# 95 | Courage without Clarity Is Hysteria

> *Clarity is the courage that doesn't need a crowd."*

It is not really about courage; it is about clarity. Courage often comes cheap. There are mental states where one appears fearless. There is nothing great about them—some greed, some weed, a bit of alcohol, hormonal excitement—and people lose all fear. Suddenly, they become heroes. In that haze, they can challenge even the god of death. Three pegs down, you ask them to jump from a seven-story building for the sake of their holy pride, and many will.

It is not courage that is the fundamental virtue. Clarity is.

There are people who are courageous, and people who are afraid. I would not greatly distinguish between them. Both operate from the same centre of ignorance. Depending on the conditions, they swing between fear and bravado.

The real distinction is between those who see and those who do not. To have clarity is to function from an entirely different centre.

# 96 | Clarity Leaves No Alternatives

> *Clarity makes the entire process of making a choice very redundant. If you know who you are and what you want, would you still be confused about the choice to make?"*

Usually, isn't decision-making such a burden on the mind? Why does one face confusion? Why does one need to think so much, often circularly? Why are there so many options? Why don't we just choicelessly know the path to take?

One sees options, and one needs to choose among them. The more the options, the greater the confusion. But what if there were no options at all? Would decision-making still be relevant, let alone tortuous?

Aren't the facts of life just obvious, indisputable, and singular? Is there an alternative to facts?

How do we manage to see options?

Maybe because I do not exactly know who I am, where I am, and how I reached here. So, I juggle between various selves. And the one with multiple selves will have multiple, competing, and contradictory desires. These desires show up as multiple options in decision-making.

## Clarity Leaves No Alternatives

The fragmentation within becomes the diversity of options one sees outside.

When you are confused about the external situation, forget the external situation for a while and turn within. Now ask: Am I watching things with dispassion and honesty, or am I watching from a centre of fear and desire?

And you will find the fog clears and the bare facts become obvious. No options, no choices, no confusion. The decision has been made.

To give eyes to a blind person is commendable. But to give sight to one with already healthy eyes is pure magic.

That is the magic we all need.

# 97 | Beyond Borrowed Light

> *The deepest enquiry begins as a tense, ruthless questioning, demanding answers, and ends in a humble surrender, knowing beyond answers."*

We don't enquire. We take things for granted.

Some old religious man said something, so it must be true.

A billionaire, a president, a celebrity, a guru proclaims something, so we believe it.

There is a tradition in the family or the company, a custom in the culture, so we honour it.

But do we ever go fearlessly to the fact? Do we ever really look?

We live in hopes, beliefs, dogmas. Our vision is clouded, not by darkness, but by borrowed light.

Ask yourself: What is all this?

All hell might be breaking loose. The world may be crashing around you.

Crowds may be shrieking in panic, rushing in every direction.

The forces of blind confidence may be stampeding.

Don't join them.

Stop.

Stand still.

Ask: What is all this?

Ask: Where is this coming from?

Your mind may be burning with desire or rage. You may feel utterly convinced that you must act.

But don't just say: *This is what I want to do.*

Ask: What exactly is happening here? Where are these impulses coming from? Do I truly know what I am doing?

And when you open your mouth to speak, ask: What have I just said? Do I even understand these words?

And then, without effort, you are home.

Because the moment real enquiry begins, the mind relaxes.

Not into laziness, but into its natural state—clear, luminous peace.

# 98 | Most 'Scriptures' Are Just Old Books

> *Spirituality addresses the unchanging essence of the 'I,' rather than fleeting beliefs, rituals, or cultural norms. True scripture explores the eternal questions of existence and identity, not rules of conduct or transient ideologies."*

Whatever belongs to time will change, and is therefore undependable. Real spirituality seeks the unchanging, the only reliable. Rites, rituals, costumes, myths, all shift with the centuries. They cannot be the target of true enquiry.

Real scriptures are not manuals about what to wear, what to eat, how to behave, or what to believe. If someone dispenses such instructions in the name of spirituality, he is either deluded or deliberately deceiving. A book of stories, codes, or belief systems is unworthy of being called a scripture.

A scripture is sacred only when it goes straight to the fundamental questions: What is existence? Who am I?

Spirituality is about the core concerns of human life, concerns that belong to everyone, everywhere: the young, the old, the African,

## Most 'Scriptures' Are Just Old Books

the American, the Indian, the Chinese, the man, the woman, the rich, the poor.

We all long for security.

We all crave companionship.

We all fear loneliness.

We desire power. We burn with jealousy.

These questions were important yesterday. They remain important today. Spirituality addresses them.

It doesn't matter what the 'I' is attached to. You might call yourself an atheist, yet you still say: *I am an atheist.* The 'I' remains. Spirituality doesn't care whether you wear the badge of belief or disbelief. It goes straight into the 'I', the only doorway to Truth.

Not every old, revered book is a scripture. And if it isn't even real, can it be sacred? Sacredness is not found in beliefs or stories. Truth, and the enquiry into it alone, is sacred.

Most old books are just outdated manuals of man's fantasies. They belong in museums, not in places of worship.

# 99 | If Truth Hurts, Niceness Kills

> *A 'nice' person tells you what you want to hear. A truthful person tells you what you need to hear. There is love in truth, and violence hidden in niceness."*

Such fools we are. We crave 'nice' people, and if someone isn't nice, we assume they don't love us. We're ready to sell our lives to anyone who will whisper two sweet lies into our ears.

But what is this niceness? Vague impressions and borrowed instincts may suffice for animals. Human beings need clarity.

*Oh, he is my friend.*

Why?

*Because he talks sweetly. He hugs me and says, 'Baba, how are you?' So nice! And since I live only on the surface, that's enough for me.*

And then there's another: who scolds, exposes, speaks plainly. I'll hate him, because he unmasks my foolishness.

Imagine a doctor telling you: *You have cancer.* Is he your enemy? Yet look at our stupidity: we'd prefer he smile and say: *All fine, dude. Go home and party.*

Isn't the whole idea of niceness disturbingly vague? Yet we cling to these fuzzy comforts, just to continue living with pleasant lies. Does that help you grow?

Real goodness is very different. But to know what is good, you must first see how rotten your current state is. Goodness means freedom from the filth clinging within and without. And that freedom is neither automatic nor painless. It demands that you peel off the layers of junk you've long called your 'self.'

Goodness is worth everything. But the price? The courage to watch your illusions burn.

Does it hurt? Yes.

That's why real goodness rarely feels nice.

# 100 | Outer Knowledge, Inner Darkness

> *The defining characteristic of real education is that it liberates you from within.*

Over the eighteen or twenty-five years of your education, what have you really studied? Languages, History, Politics, Geography, Economy. And Maths and Physics and Chemistry. A flood of facts, formulas, maps, and dates.

But here's the uncomfortable question: Are you the English or French language? Are you a chemical equation or a geometry theorem? Are you the rivers and glaciers printed in your textbooks? Are you Alexander or Ashoka? Are you hardware? Are you code?

Clearly, all this you have been taught about is something *outside* you. And that's exactly what mainstream education gives you: information about the world, about external objects.

But you are not an object. You are the subject. You are not outside yourself. You are the one who reads, who thinks, who cries, who chooses, who suffers, who longs.

So why have you not studied *yourself*? Has your education ever brought you closer to your own centre? Has it ever helped you understand your mind? Your patterns? Your attachments? Your fears? Has it ever asked the questions: *What is love? What is freedom of mind? What does it mean to live consciously? Who am I?*

## Outer Knowledge, Inner Darkness

I ask you now, what is more important: all the polished objects around you, or *You*?

We live in a world where objects are smart, shiny, sophisticated, and man is lost, confused, violent, ugly. Please Google: 'Sixth Mass Extinction.' What is the use of holding the most advanced phone in your hand, if it only amplifies your inner noise? In the hands of a blind mind, is the phone a tool or a toxin?

We've taught machines how to think. But forgot to ask: Can we think? Yes, we've achieved great scientific feats. But what have we done with them? We mass-produce. We over-consume. We burn. We poison. We devastate. And we call this achievement. What has made this possible?

*Education.*

Education that knows everything about the world, but nothing about the one *who is knowing* it. Education that forgets to ask: *What is it to be human? What is attention? What is the nature of thought?*

This is not education. This is training. Programming. Conditioning. True education begins when the student is no longer seen as a machine to be filled, but as a being to be awakened.

I say this again, and will keep saying it till my last breath: If all your formal education is placed on one side, and **self-education**—education of the Self—on the other, then self-education is infinitely more valuable. Because only self-education can liberate. And liberation is the only real goal of learning.

# 101 | Slaves of Approval, Strangers to Truth

> *Fundamentally, you are not enslaved by the other. You are enslaved by your own fear and greed. There are no other masters!"*

Even the most intimate, sacred centres of your life are ruled by a single, suffocating question: *What will they think?* You speak because others are watching. And you stay silent because others are watching. Their gaze becomes your cage. Directly or indirectly, consciously or unconsciously, the shadow of the other dominates your life.

Why? Because you believe yourself to be what others say you are. You live in reflection, not in reality. Someone calls you "wonderful," and suddenly you feel elevated. Not because you have seen your truth, but because you are starving, and any crumb of approval feels like a feast. But in that moment of sweetness, you do not notice the poison: you've surrendered your centre to someone else.

The same lips that praised you in the morning can damn you by evening. And if their morning compliment lifted you, their evening insult will crush you. This is slavery. And it happens only because you do not know who you are. When you are conscious and clear, the opinions of others become irrelevant. But without that clarity, you grovel. You beg—subtly, politely, constantly—for validation, for certification, for a sign that you are enough.

Even in your closest relationships, you live behind a mask. You perform versions of yourself to be liked, to be accepted. And what's worse? You call it love. That's not love, that's fear in disguise. That's cowardice dressed as intimacy.

Ever truly observed a real child? A two-month-old doesn't hesitate. If she wants to cry, she cries. She doesn't care for social niceties. You could be the President of the world; if your face displeases her, she'll slap you, dismiss you, and if you still linger, she'll soil your precious suit without guilt or delay.

That was you, once: before the chains were wrapped around your mind. Before you were trained to doubt yourself. Before you were domesticated. Before you were taught to behave.

So what happened?

You picked up hesitation. You picked up shame. You picked up masks. Somewhere along the way, when you were most vulnerable and hungry for belonging, you were taught to trade truth for approval.

Yes, society exploited the child in you. Yes, you were conditioned. Mostly unknowingly. But the fact remains: the damage was done. Now the question is: must it continue? The past has passed. The cage door is open. The only question is: will you step out? Or will you keep kneeling before shadows, calling them your masters?

# 102 | Missing the Obvious

> *You are not missing the secret; you are missing the obvious."*

Something very obvious happens right in front of you, and yet you fail to see through it.

The plain, everyday occurrences—greeting someone, walking to work, hearing a passing comment—carry you away without resistance. Things penetrate our inner world without our consent.

Why do the most ordinary things succeed so effortlessly in deceiving us?

Because we are not really available to the fact of things. We are not present to what objects, events, and people actually are. We don't look at them directly. We don't listen to what they are saying, here and now.

Instead, we are preoccupied, mentally elsewhere. Engaged with inner distortions, with chosen fragments and echoes from the past.

We filter everything through stale memories and learned impressions. So what's happening in the foreground, here and now, gets drowned in the background noise.

Our reactions are based on history, not reality.

## Missing the Obvious

This blindness is not due to the complexity of happenings. It's due to our refusal to look directly at them. To really observe what is happening, without lenses.

The act of seeing is not complicated. In fact, it is so straightforward that the mind resists it. It appears too simple, too bare.

We expect a secret, a mystery, a technique. But truth doesn't hide, it just doesn't shout. It is there for you, and you decide whether to acknowledge it.

Nothing is easier than pure observation:

looking without assumption,

listening without agenda,

perceiving without fear.

It asks for nothing special, just sincerity.

And that is why its results are extraordinary.

# 103 | Laughing at Your Own Idiocy

> *Beginning to see one's foolishness is the beginning of wisdom."*

You must pass through the full spectrum of human experience.

Maddening anger, irresistible lust, the terrible compulsion to be dishonest: these are not anomalies. They are forces of nature. They arise not because you are flawed, but because you are alive. To be human is to encounter them.

At some point or another, these forces will grip you. And when they do, don't deny them. Don't suppress, don't distort, and most importantly, don't disguise.

Call dishonesty dishonesty. Call lust lust. Call anger anger, shame shame. Don't sugarcoat your inner state with clever names like "passion" or "strategy" or "self-defense."

Stand naked. Stand firm. See what you truly are in that moment.

And when you've walked through it—without masks, without excuses—you must be able to laugh. Laugh not with arrogance, but with lightness. Even better, if you can laugh while still caught in the middle of it. That means a subtle distance has begun. You are beginning to witness yourself.

That's progress.

Blessed is the one who can say: *You know what, I was such an idiot.*

Absolutely blessed is the one who can say: *You know what, I am an idiot.*

That is the collapse of vanity. That is the moment when wisdom peeks through.

And if you can't say, "I am an idiot" yet, then at least say, "I was an idiot." That's a good beginning.

Begin there, and keep walking.

# 104 | The Power of Collective Stupidity

> *When the Truth is decided by the verdict of the masses, falseness reigns. Put truth to a vote, and falseness takes the throne."*

Stupidity, on its own, is weak. It can be crushed easily. But stupidity knows its weakness, so it gathers numbers. It builds associations, flags, slogans, parliaments, and platforms.

One fool is dismissed. A million fools become a movement and then a government. Now stupidity is no longer an error. It is an institution.

If one man wants socks with a thousand holes, he is declared mad. But if a million want them, there will be a market, a ministry, a manifesto. Anyone questioning the madness will be branded the real problem.

That is how falseness survives. Not through merit, but through multiplication.

Truth does not need numbers. It does not need approval. It does not seek comfort. It stands alone.

But falseness? It craves applause. It feeds on the crowd. It thrives in the marketplace of minds that refuse to think.

## The Power of Collective Stupidity

And when stupidity becomes collective, it becomes holy. Now it is not just ignorance, it is identity. It is custom. It is democracy.

Evil does not always arrive as a tyrant. Sometimes, it marches in as the will of the people. Because the greatest evil often lies in the great number of small people.

# 105 | Wake Up before You Die

> *The purpose of life lies in the process of living – live with clarity, love freedom."*

With each breath, with each passing day, you must deepen: not in possessions, not in information, but in understanding. You must grow lighter, not heavier. Freer, not more entangled.

Real growth is not about acquiring. It is about shedding. Shedding illusions, shedding borrowed dreams, shedding the false self you mistook as 'you'.

You were born with ignorance. You must not die with it.

You were born with tendencies. You must not carry them to the grave.

When death comes, it should not be the end of a confused journey: it should be the completion of a sacred one. A summit reached. A knot untied.

To die rightly is to die having lived rightly. It is to die unburdened, unbound, and fulfilled.

That is success. Not in what you achieved, but in what you dissolved.

# SOCIETY AND THE GAME OF OTHERS

# 106 | Gossip Bonds the Insecure

> *Gossip provides a false sense of connection, helping insecure minds bond over shared trivialities to mask their deeper fears."*

The family of nonsense is vast. It offers warmth, inclusion, a cozy illusion of togetherness. But stepping out of it demands something most people lack: the courage to face their inner emptiness.

Two or three people are gossiping, and soon three more join in, and then three more. What brings them together? What binds them? Not truth. Not clarity. Just nonsense. That's the strange comfort nonsense offers: it helps people feel connected.

Why do we crave that connection? Because we are insecure. And instead of confronting that insecurity, we mask it by clinging to others, others who are equally unsure, equally hollow, and equally loud.

*Verma talks nonsense, Sharma talks nonsense, Chopra talks nonsense. So if I talk nonsense, I belong. I'm part of the tribe. It feels warm. It feels safe. It feels like family.*

But drop the nonsense, and the door shuts. You are now excluded. You no longer belong. And with that comes exposure. Vulnerability.

Aloneness. That's when one needs inner strength: faith, honesty, and the capacity to be free without belonging.

Most people don't want that. So they stay. In noise. In triviality. In the comfort of false connection. And that's why the family of nonsense is so huge.

# 107 | Live Healthy in a Sick World

> *Remember the principle:*
> *You become the one you look up to.*
> *You become the one who occupies*
> *your time. You become the one*
> *who occupies your mind."*

It is impossible not to notice that we are living in a very sick world. What you read in the newspapers is sick. What you see around you is sick. The marketplaces, the malls, the entertainment, the education system, the political discourse, all are soaked in confusion and disease. Suffering is not the exception; it is the background noise of our lives.

Turn on the television. What do you find? Do you see silence, depth, clarity? Or do you see the same restless game: ambition, insecurity, competition, greed, jealousy, possession? The same madness dressed in a thousand colors, calling itself success, romance, growth, power.

It may be disappointing. It may even be revolting. But it is also real. This is the world we live in. And if you are constantly surrounded by sickness, it will creep into you. Influence is subtle. The one who occupies your attention begins to occupy your being.

But even if the world is that rotten, the question remains: do you want to live like that? Do you want to become part of that noise, just because it's everywhere? Do you want to let the filth outside dictate your inner life?

If the answer is no, then the purpose of life becomes very clear. The purpose must be to live healthily in the midst of all this illness. To remain inwardly untouched. To defend inner clarity even if it means standing alone. To gain health, and if needed, to protect that health at the cost of your very life.

And then, naturally, to bring that health to others. To become a point of light in this dark flood. Not because the world needs saving, but because the healthy one radiates. Healing flows through him— not as effort, but as his very nature.

This is not charity. This is not morality. This is not some noble mission. It is simply what you owe yourself.

# 108 | Give Yourself a Second Birth

> *True growth requires a second birth: through self-knowledge, education, and freedom from the instincts we inherit.*

A human being is not born. A human being must be made.

Strange as it may sound, humanness is not a birthright. It is not given by biology. It is not a consequence of coming out of the womb. It is a possibility: one that must be awakened, cultivated, and realized.

At birth, we are merely bodies with potential. Within us are embedded the seeds of ignorance, greed, lust, fear, jealousy. We are born with these forces, not above them. Unless something intervenes, unless there is an inner revolution, our life will be nothing but the fulfillment of our biological script. We will chase what the body demands. We will live and die without knowing who we are.

That's why every human child needs two births. One physical, the other psychological. The first comes from the mother; the second must come from truth, from understanding.

This is what true education must do, it must liberate. It must help us see the patterns we are trapped in. Not just train the mind to store facts, but show the mind how it has become its own prison. To be educated is not to have a degree. It is to be inwardly free.

Academic knowledge may help us survive, but it cannot help us live rightly. Right living begins only when there is self-awareness. Real learning means you are able to observe your own inner machinery—your reactions, fears, attractions—and gently step out of the rut.

That is why education is not just for school. It is a lifelong process. To be truly alive is to be learning always: to be constantly shedding false identities, breaking inner bondages, and moving toward clarity.

Without this second birth, man remains a creature of instinct. With it, he becomes a conscious being.

# 109 | When Success Fails the Self

> *You must clearly enquire to what extent all your worldly endeavours have actually nurtured your inner well-being.*

When we talk of external growth, what does it usually mean? We earn, we accumulate, we gain knowledge and experience. All this is called growth, and that is fine in itself. But alongside it, we must keep asking: For whom is this accumulation? Whose welfare are we serving by gathering money, power, and achievements?

When you ask this question, the whole picture shifts. Obviously, we do not earn money or knowledge for their own sake. We do it for ourselves, for our own well-being.

So, this question—*for whom?*—is critical. When you look closely, you see that even your external striving is centred on you, the seeker, the striver. And like any process that consumes effort and time, this process must be measured against its ultimate output: the welfare of the inner self.

You see, we are born with certain tendencies that do not let us be at peace. Even a newborn carries rudimentary fear, greed, and ignorance. As life proceeds, social conditioning only deepens these tendencies. We gather experiences, opinions, and codes of right and wrong, most of which do not help our inner growth.

Internally, we all begin with a mess. That chaos must be cleaned. That is inner growth.

Inner growth is the reduction of inner clutter, not the addition of new baggage. And external growth is only meaningful if it serves this inner cleansing.

# 110 | Not Every Crime Screams

> *Society's concern for women suddenly peaks during headline crimes, but real change demands attention to the silent suffering of their everyday life."*

Beyond the horror of sensational crimes, there lies a quiet and constant erosion, a systemic violence that never makes it to the news.

A woman isn't allowed to work after marriage, nobody bats an eyelid.

She faces harassment at work, it's considered part of the job.

She dies during childbirth, just a statistic.

She cannot walk safely through public spaces, that's not even discussed.

She is conditioned to see her body as her identity, everyone approves.

She is underrepresented in professional education and leadership, but who cares?

She is murdered, and it's a two-inch column in the local newspaper.

But let there be a brutal rape case, and suddenly there's nationwide outrage. Rightly so. Rape is an unspeakable violation. But the question is, what exactly are we outraged at?

Are we grieving the woman's pain, or are we feeding on the lurid details?

Let's be honest. In most cases, it is not justice most people want, it is titillation. It is not the woman we stand for, it is the drama that excites us. And once the noise fades, nothing changes.

If we truly cared, we would not wait for a rape to be shocked into attention. We would notice the daily exploitation, the structural oppression, the silent brutality of conditioning that women are forced to swallow. We would act not just when a headline demands it, but when a woman is denied dignity in the smallest of ways.

Real concern begins with asking:

Have we raised our daughters to inquire into their freedom?

Have we given them the tools to think independently, to reject the roles imposed upon them, to walk out of systems that do not serve their inner welfare?

Until that happens, all our outrage is performance. And the real violence—silent, subtle, systemic—continues.

# 111 | They Sell You the Wound, Then the Cure

> "The broken ones first convince you that you're broken, then sell you a cure that convinces you deeper."

Why do most people work? Because they are dissatisfied with themselves. Dissatisfaction is the fuel. So if someone wants to make you work for them, or as per their desires, what must they do? They must first deepen your dissatisfaction. They must convince you: *You're not enough as you are. Something is wrong with you.*

And then they offer you a promise: *Work the way we tell you, chase the success we define, buy the things we sell, and only then will you be fulfilled.* That's how they get hold of your inner reins. They first implant a sense of lack, then they sell you the solution. And you, precious and capable, spend your life running after what they've made you desire.

You've been conditioned this way for years. Family, school, society, religion: each told you that something is missing in you, and that you must earn your worth. You were not taught to be at peace with yourself. You were made to feel small. Even love became conditional: *You don't deserve it unless you succeed.* Your identity became a performance, measured in applause.

That's where the damage began.

But hear this clearly: there is nothing fundamentally wrong with you. You are not lacking. Your gossip, your restlessness, your anxiety: they all come from this implanted lie that you are incomplete.

Drop that notion.

You are already whole. Even with your limitations, you are radiant. Even buried under layers of conditioning, you remain precious. A diamond in the mud doesn't lose its worth. You are that diamond.

But those who don't know their own value spend their lives making others feel worthless. There are only two kinds of people: those who have accepted smallness, and those who dance in completeness. The ones who feel small are always trying to shrink others. The frightened can't help but spread fear.

But completeness is not a dream. It is your nature. It may be buried, but it has never left you.

Uncover it.

The purpose of life is not to run pitifully after things in search of completion. It is to uncover the wholeness already within, and to live from it, fearlessly, beautifully, lovingly.

# 112 | Sacred Dissatisfaction

> *"You have one life. Never settle down. Keep aiming for a self higher than the highest you have known."*

We have an unfortunate tendency: we make peace with our circumstances. Not because they are right, but because they are familiar. We settle wherever chance drops us. We adjust to mediocrity. We justify stagnation.

You won't find many who are deeply dissatisfied with life. On the surface, people complain about stress, systems and others. But underneath, there is often quiet comfort with the wrong life. True discontent, the kind that demands transformation, is rare.

We settle. We accept. We compromise. The urge to break free, to rise, to disrupt one's own comfort, is missing. The tragedy is not that we suffer, but that we stay where we suffer, pretending it's fine.

But just as settling becomes a habit, so can not settling. You can cultivate a different instinct: the instinct to move, to renew, to rebel inwardly. You can train yourself to question ease, disturb the known, challenge what's assumed.

## Sacred Dissatisfaction

Even when it seems unnecessary, even when no one else sees the need—keep moving. Keep challenging. Keep changing. Let restlessness become sacred. Let refusal become discipline.

Rise to a higher place, and don't settle even there. The journey is not toward a static peak. There is no final destination. Or perhaps, the destination is to rise forever.

# 113 | Born Animal, Meant to Rise

> *Everybody is biologically an animal, but why must one remain an animal psychologically? The physical animal need not be suppressed, but the inner animal must be transcended."*

Observe animals attentively. What you see in them is what you must question in yourself. Whatever is common between you and them is not to be accepted: it is to be seen and gone beyond.

Animals are jealous. Jealousy guards territory, wins mates, hoards food. They deceive, attack, submit: tools for survival in the wild.

They form bonds, but out of instinct, not awareness. They manipulate. They compete. They use violence and trickery. These are responses to danger, not choices.

Now ask: Do you need jealousy to earn a living? Deception to breathe? Violence to survive?

If not, why carry these traits? Why defend them as natural?

Yes, you're born in a body. But you're not just a body. You don't have to live by jungle logic.

Let the body do what it must. But the mind must rise. The inner animal must be seen and released.

# 114 | Not Toward Each Other, but Upward

> *Relationships are great only when they help elevate your consciousness, and that's the only purpose of relationships in life."*

If you're with someone, check one thing. It will tell you everything about your relationship: Is that person drawing you toward himself, or guiding you toward your own betterment?

If his presence makes you orbit around his moods, his needs, his validations, he is not your well-wisher. If he wants to be your top priority, if he demands your attention more than he encourages your growth, he is not worthy of being your partner.

The self-interest and subtle violence in ordinary love should be visible, if you're even slightly alert. Most relationships are rooted in emotional dependence, not in mutual elevation.

A person is a worthy partner only if he sees that what you truly need is not his body, not his company for comfort, but light and liberation.

With such a partner, the journey is not toward each other. It is not about merging or losing oneself in the other. It is about walking together, side by side, toward freedom.

Isn't that love? Not possession, not obsession, but shared clarity and mutual ascent.

# 115 | Do They Love You— or Limit You?

> *If your pursuit of greatness hurts those around you, it only shows their desire to keep you chained to their smallness."*

If others feel wounded by your aspirations, is it love? Or do they simply want you trapped in their limitations?

If you move toward greatness, or aspire for it, and that hurts the people around you, it means that those people intend to remain small.

It also means they do not love you. In truth, they are hostile. They don't just refuse to walk with you, they want to block your path.

In love, you want the highest for the other, even at your own cost. If someone close to you moves toward liberation, and you feel hurt or insecure, you are not their well-wisher.

Smallness is bondage. Greatness is freedom.

Who is your enemy? The one invested in keeping you small.

# 116 | Jealousy: The Pain of Borrowed Identity

> *"Jealousy is the ache of a self borrowed from others. Jealousy thrives where self-knowing is absent."*

What exactly is the ego? It is the sense of myself, borrowed from others. I do not know who I am directly. I depend on somebody else to tell me.

A fellow comes and says, *You are brilliant,* and I start believing I am brilliant. My self-image now hangs on this other person. He told me I am brilliant; therefore I am.

The opposite is also inevitable. If they come and tell me I am stupid, I have to believe that too. Even my idea of stupidity comes from others. If I accept their praise, I must accept their criticism.

My brilliance does not arise from my understanding. My sense of self is borrowed. I crave their approval. The more they endorse me, the more special I feel.

So far so good. But what happens the day I see them praising someone else? I will not like it. My identity feels threatened. The source that lent me my existence as a brilliant one is now turning away. This threat to my dependent identity is jealousy.

## Jealousy: The Pain of Borrowed Identity

Now take a different situation. I know that I am brilliant. My understanding is my own. It is not a borrowed idea. Will I still be jealous when someone else is praised? No.

Jealousy is born from dependence. The one who is not dependent is free of jealousy. The one who is his own master cannot be jealous.

Jealousy, in that sense, is the pain of being a slave to others. If you want to be free of jealousy, see clearly where you are leaning on others to define yourself.

# 117 | Technology Isn't the Problem, You Are

> *Solve your mind, all other problems will be solved."*

Blind consumption is annihilation: for you, for other species, for the planet. And consumption cannot be checked unless you address the consumer. By consumer, I don't mean the one with money. I mean the ego. Unless the ego is seen and understood, nothing else will change.

Technology will keep advancing, and it should. Even if you legislate against progress, curiosity won't disappear. Exploration is human nature. We will keep probing what lies beyond.

The trouble is, our curiosity rarely turns inward. Even our endless investigation of the world is a disguised search for the self. We want to know who we are, so we keep dissecting everything around us.

The real question is: Who is consuming this science? With what intention is a technology developed? For what purpose does money fund research? Nuclear energy can light a city, or flatten it.

Is the knower wise? Is the consumer sane? Because supply will keep overflowing. Markets will expand. Products will multiply. The question is: Are we ready?

You cannot stop supply. You must awaken demand. You cannot stop shops from selling goods, but you can awaken the buyer. When the consumer transforms, the producer must follow. If wisdom doesn't guide the seller, market failure eventually will.

Educate the masses. Awaken intelligence in the ordinary person. No other solution will work.

# 118 | Good Spirituality Is Good Economics

> *A thing is only as valuable as its utility or ability to bring its user to an inner fulfillment. In absence of self-awareness, there is a big gap between the price and value of things.*

We relate to external objects for inner fulfillment. A thing is only as valuable as its ability to bring peace, clarity, and elevation to the one using it.

Without self-awareness, we often mistake price for value. That is the beginning of individual sorrow and collective ruin.

All economics ultimately exists for human well-being. But what is human well-being? It is the upliftment of consciousness. If something does not serve that purpose, it is not valuable, no matter how costly or widely demanded it may be.

Why must value be rooted in the inner life? Because even the outer, for humans, derives its meaning from the inner. A disturbed man surrounded by luxuries remains miserable. What use are goods and comforts if they fail to nourish the self?

That is why real value begins within. When your consciousness is dense, impure, and restless, you won't even know what deserves value. You will buy junk, sell your soul, and chase distractions. But when consciousness is clear, even your market choices become sacred.

What does it mean to lift consciousness? It means to rise above compulsions: ignorance, delusion, instinct. It means to break free of being merely a product of conditioning.

And once that happens, you start asking the right question: not "how much does it cost?," but "what does it do to my mind?"

That is how all goods and services must be evaluated:

Does it uplift me inwardly? If yes, buy it, even at a high price.

Does it corrupt me inwardly? If yes, discard it, even if it comes for free.

Real economics is not separate from real spirituality. A pure market is one that aligns with a pure mind.

# 119 | Love Reflects the Self

> *Beauty and greatness do not come by accident. They have to be earned, achieved through sustained practice. You must pay the price.*

Who are you?

You say, *I am X*.

Are you?

*I am*.

This *I* is what you really are. In every declaration of identity, this *I* comes first. The labels keep changing, but the one claiming them remains the same. This *I* is the self.

The quality of your life is simply the quality of this *I*. All your relationships spring from it. If the self is clean, relationships will be clean. If the self is corrupt, relationships will be corrupt.

The depth of love, the courage to be truthful, the freedom to live simply, all depend on the condition of this self.

If the self is innocent and clear, relationships are direct and loving. If it is tangled in fear, ignorance, and conditioning, relationships will drip with greed, demands, and insecurity.

## Love Reflects the Self

Do you want love that is genuine? Clean up the self. Do you want to feel whole and unafraid? Clean up the self.

Who will do this cleaning? The self itself.

How will it happen? By seeing how soiled it has become.

How do you come to that seeing? By observing the self in action. The self is known through its movements.

Where do these movements show? In feelings, thoughts, words, gestures.

Fear, anger, craving, ambition, all these are actions of the self as much as walking or speaking.

When you watch them without bias, you come to know the real state of your mind. And that very seeing is transformative. For the self, diagnosis is the cure.

We all wish to have great relationships, deep love, and clean companionship. But these are not possible without first working on yourself. Self-knowledge is the foundation. The only way. The wayless way.

# 120 | Where Rape Really Begins

> *All forms of cruelty share the same root. Whether it is rape, genocide, or the extinction of species, they all arise from the same barren soil: the absence of love, the absence of awareness, the abundance of ignorance.*

Is rape just an isolated sexual event? Or is it a process, an accumulating violence that finally erupts in a grotesque climax?

We are trained to see the world as something to consume. Our ideas of progress and happiness often revolve around grabbing more, owning more, destroying more. This is not just economics. This is mindset.

Consider simple contact. When you touch someone or something, what is the intention? To nourish, or to extract pleasure? Is there any love in that touch?

How far is loveless, self-serving contact from exploitation, mental, physical, or sexual? The line is thin. Too thin.

We must stop treating rape as an isolated horror. If we are serious about ending it, we must understand how it grows: in homes, in films, in politics, in jokes, in silences.

Look around: our rivers choked, forests scraped bare, hill stations buried under plastic, species vanishing without names. What is this if not collective rape: of nature, of dignity, of the sacred?

Where there is power without love, technology without awareness, contact without reverence, abuse follows. And when abuse becomes a way of life, rape is not an aberration. It is a culmination.

What is needed is not just punishment, but purification. Not just reaction, but revolution in the way we live, touch, relate, desire.

We need an education that doesn't merely prepare us to earn or argue, but to love rightly. Only that will end this madness.

# 121 | The Third Woman

> *True feminism begins when a woman is liberated from the physical and social compulsion to take her body as her primary identity."*

First, there was the woman shaped by patriarchy feeding on biology—raised to be pleasing, compliant, decorative, dainty. She was taught her worth lay in her body, in her ability to gratify expectations.

Then came the second woman, the rebel. She was furious at the power and pride of men. But in her rebellion, she ended up becoming their reflection. She wore like men. She smoked like men. She talked like men. She chased success like men. And she remained, or became, just as restless and unconscious as men.

So what really changed?

The slave became a mirror of the master. The reaction became a repetition. The rebellion became mimicry.

But there is a third woman possible. She is not an imitation. She is not a reaction. She is not defined by what she opposes or what she copies. She is a human being. She is consciousness first—and only much later, a body.

She watches her impulses without glorifying them. She sees her patterns without being enslaved. She does not identify. She does not submit. She witnesses.

Her aim is not equality with men. Her aim is liberation. Her goal is not to seize power, but to discover truth.

She does not exist to remain a prisoner of biology or culture. She exists to let her consciousness express its highest potential.

This is the woman the world desperately needs. Not the woman of tradition. Not the woman of reaction. But the woman of realization.

Much of this world's confusion, violence, and sorrow will begin to heal the day more women discover this third possibility.

# 122 | The Industry of Incompleteness

> *"The usual 'motivation' is nothing but the illusion of inadequacy, fueled by a society that convinces you you're missing something essential."*

You've been told you're incomplete. So you chase degrees, promotions, partners, possessions, trying to fill a void that may never have existed in the first place.

Motivation thrives on fear, on comparison, on shame. How else will they sell you their cures, their creams, their dreams, if they don't first make you feel broken?

They make you feel broken, then sell you their fixes.

That's not motivation. That's manipulation.

At the root of the word 'motivation' is 'motive'. And what is a motive? *I want something I don't have.* Which means: *I am not enough.*

That is the lie. That is the poison.

From every corner—family, media, culture, religion—you are told:

Look at uncle's son.

You are useless without a man.

## The Industry of Incompleteness

No child? You're barren.

Only one? Have two.

Two-bedroom flat? Aim for a villa.

Then you'll be complete.

This is not love. This is not care. This is corruption. This is violence.

They first convince you that you are inadequate. Once you have bought that, then they can sell you anything.

They first sell you the disease. Then they sell you the desire to heal. Is that not what most of our desires are – an attempt to remedy a problem that may not exist in the first place?

So your ambition, your motivation, your goals: they do not arise from understanding. They are born from fear, from a wound that was planted in you, from a sense of lack that was never yours to begin with.

And so you keep running. Not toward something real, but away from yourself.

Motivation is not a sign of strength. It is the noise of a mind that doesn't know itself. It is the desperation of someone trying to become, because they've forgotten they already are.

Real action does not come from motivation. It comes from clarity. From inwardness. From seeing that there is nothing wrong with you.

You don't need motivation. You need liberation.

# 123 | The Emotional Engine of Climate Collapse

> "Our primitive instincts arise from the center of the jungle. And they end up destroying the jungle. A climate of wisdom inside is the only way to restore the climate outside."

When we don't operate from a center of wisdom, we operate from a center of blind emotion. And these emotions, as strange as it may sound, are fuelling climate change.

One is so emotional about that next foreign holiday. That longing itself is carbon, every climate report shows this. Tourism and aviation are massive contributors to emissions.

One feels emotional about having a beautiful, secure nest of his own. That too is carbon. Deforestation, urbanisation, cement, steel: our ancient cravings demand them all.

One feels emotional about raising a picture-perfect family with two lovely kids. That too is emotion, and that too is carbon. The fundamental driver of the ecological crisis is the unrestrained rise in the human population, rooted in unchecked desire.

Look closely. Every time we surrender to emotion, in some direct or indirect way, we become a carbon emitter.

## The Emotional Engine of Climate Collapse

Don't the sellers arouse our emotions to make us binge on shopping? When your vision is clouded by feeling, it becomes easier to make you spend senselessly and celebrate mindlessly.

We demand constant emotional stimulation. All of it adds to the burden on the planet.

It is astonishing that so many who loudly claim to care about the environment refuse to see that the climate crisis is, at its core, a crisis of unexamined emotionality. Emotions left unchecked are the hunger that will devour this earth.

And the antidote is wisdom.

Wisdom is nothing but the honest understanding of the self and its restless impulses. Wisdom alone can look into the roots of our greed and fear, our need to consume and possess.

Wait: Are we talking about killing emotion here? No. We are talking about the light of wisdom that purifies emotion.

From the centre of clarity, emotion is not merely beautiful, it is sacred.

Right emotion arises from the right centre of being. That inner individual illumined centre alone can save the planet – not just governmental policy or green technology.

# 124 | Parent, First Raise Yourself

> *"To really raise a child, you must first raise yourself."*

Take care of yourself—truly, deeply—and you've already taken care of your child. When a child lives with a radiant mother, a radiant father, their fears dissolve without a lesson being taught. Your presence teaches more than your words ever can.

Your first duty is not to fix the child. It is to awaken yourself. Because if your mind is wounded, conflicted, and dark, then that is all you will pass on. You may pretend to be loving, but your unconsciousness will seep through every touch, every glance, every word unspoken.

Yet this is the strange irony of parenting. We cling to our darkness and still dream of gifting light to our children. We remain unhealed and still hope to be healers. That is not parenting. That is delusion.

You cannot give what you do not have. You cannot teach what you do not live. You cannot guide from confusion and fear. And that's why parents across generations have failed.

They want their children to be free, but they themselves live in bondage. They want their children to be joyful, while they carry a face carved by sorrow. They want their children to be conscious, but haven't taken a single step toward consciousness themselves.

You cannot hand over light when your own hands are full of shadows.

So if you truly love your child, stop obsessing over their future. Begin with your own inner revolution.

Raise your awareness. Raise your integrity. Raise your life.

Because only when the parent rises does the child get wings.

And then, without effort, your very being becomes a sanctuary. Your silence becomes scripture. Your life becomes their greatest blessing.

Don't raise your child from habit. Raise them from awakening.

And for that, you must awaken first.

# 125 | The Holy Eight-Step Suicide

> *Walking down the same beaten lane, how will you ever come to a new destination?"*

You're not lost. You're on a highway: smooth, polished, well-lit. And that's the problem. We're all treading the same certified path: be born, get educated, get a job, get married, buy a house, buy a car, raise kids, argue with your spouse, maybe divorce, maybe remarry, grow old, die.

The holy eight-step process to death. A conveyor belt dressed up as life.

And the tragedy? Most of us are already halfway through. Four steps done, four more to go. But we still live in denial. *No, no,* we insist, *my life is different. Paradise is waiting for me!* Such comforting delusion.

We want to feel special. We want to believe that the same road which led billions into quiet frustration and respectable despair will somehow take us to bliss. Same direction, same vehicle, same fuel—yet we imagine ourselves heading to a different destination? On what basis?

You are not walking your path. You are just walking the default. And the default has only one destination: unconscious consumption, shallow success, inner hollowness, and finally, death without ever having lived.

If you want a new destination, you must take a new path. And for that, you must first stop walking. Stand still. Ask. Turn around. The beaten path doesn't take you forward. It beats you down.

# SUFFERING: THE GATE TO SINCERITY

# 126 | Even Wounds Can Smile

> *Pain is inevitable, but it can be seen with wisdom, and hence transcended."*

Welcome pain. You have no option. Pain will be a recurring visitor, that is the very nature of life.

Life is suffering, because not only are we designed to have pain, we are also designed to resist pain. This resistance is the core of suffering.

Don't resist pain when it comes, and have a lot of depth in your being—so much depth that it can take in all the pain.

If you resist pain, all you get is suffering. This suffering is not the pain itself, but the ego's futile rebellion against what is.

If you embrace pain, then there is a silent power. You see that you can take it all, that you are strong beyond the vagaries of circumstances.

If you can smile through tears, and in tears—what a beautiful smile you have! A smile not of gratification, but of realisation.

Even wounds can smile. Suffering is always a choice.

# 127 | Stop Collecting Wounds

> *Nobody can bring inner harm to you without your consent."*

Yes, people and situations can hurt you. But the harm they do is almost always small compared to the damage you inflict on yourself—by clutching it to your chest, by internalizing it, by turning it into part of your identity.

External harm remains on the periphery. It knocks, it scratches, it tries to enter, but unless you allow it, it cannot touch your core. If you're living rightly, nothing can pierce your centre. Your essence stays untouched.

It's vital to keep hurt in its place, and that place is never your heart, never your sacred interiors. Let it stay outside. Let it pass through. Don't invite it in.

If something stinky happens to you, what do you do? You wash it off and move on. You don't bottle the stink and carry it around like some precious belonging. Yet that's what most people do with emotional wounds.

If someone cheats you, it doesn't smell of roses, it reeks. Why this strange indulgence in preserving the stink? Why decorate your shelf with the memory of betrayal? Why turn pain into a personal artifact?

Drop it. Walk on. Life is not a museum of old wounds. It is not a gallery of grievances. It deserves your freshness. It demands your clarity.

Let the past rot where it belongs. Don't carry it into the sacred space of your present.

# 128 | All Is Well, until It Isn't

> *If your sense of wellness depends on something outside you, it isn't wellness, it's insecurity."*

Isn't shallow wellness just hidden pain, waiting to show up?

You must have noticed some people who are always sulking. And then, there are others who wear a constant smile and speak in that soft, sunny voice. Ask them how life is, and they quickly respond: *All is well.*

Real wellness is precious. But fake wellness is just self-deception, it's the opposite of real wellness.

Many confidently say: *Everything is perfectly fine.* They aren't lying. It's just that their sense of well-being is shallow. Yes, there is happiness, but only on the surface. Scratch it a little, and it disappears. A small setback arrives, and their calmness collapses. Cheerfulness vanishes. Worry and sadness take over.

If your wellness had real depth, would your mind break down so easily?

Ironically, these are the people who say: *I don't need wisdom. I don't need spirituality. I'm already fine.* But they are the most prone to anxiety, depression, and mental disorder.

Real happiness is wonderful. Be truly happy, joyful, alive. Even doctors will agree.

Vedanta says: *Niramayo Aham*—Wellness is my true nature.

But for that real wellness to emerge, you must do something radical. You must stop being the same person you used to be. Only then can you rise above your past.

# 129 | The Past Is the Present

> *If you don't learn from your past, it won't stay behind you, it will disguise itself as your future."*

The sorrow of the past is not something to blindly discard or erase.

People will urge you to forget. *Let go,* they say. *Live only in the present.* But that is not wisdom. That is escapism dressed as freedom.

If you want to truly live now, you must know what masquerades as the 'now'. The present is not the present, it is the past in a new mask. If the past dominates the present, then the present must be freed by confronting the past.

One never just drifts past the past. Conscious effort is needed.

Go back to the forest where your footsteps were left behind. The paths you once took, they are still alive. And they have grown on you.

Listen to what they are still whispering. Don't pretend you've outgrown their language.

The present is nothing but a shadow cast by the fires of yesterday. And tomorrow will carry the same mark, unless you intervene.

To change your course, you must unclench. Let go of the rusted anchors you've mistaken for identity.

## The Past Is the Present

You cannot dance with grace while still tangled in yesterday's knots. You cannot sing of liberation while hiding silent shame.

What you do not understand will continue to rule you. What you do not face will keep following you.

To learn is to unlock: not by fleeing, but by cleaning the wound instead of covering it.

It is to meet yourself honestly, not dramatically.

Understanding doesn't just free you from what happened. It frees you from who you thought you were because of it.

# 130 | Stop Choosing Misery

> *The world will appear to provoke you, control you, and shake you. If you are deeply rooted in wisdom, you remain untouched."*

Stress is a fact of life. The body and mind have evolved in a field of tension. They are built to experience stress, at least in doses.

But you must know yourself as something prior to the body and the mind. That real self must stand unshaken even as storms pass through.

In your natural state, you must love joy so fiercely that you simply refuse to let stress breach your inner sanctuary.

When stress begins to violate your intrinsic joy, it should feel like being torn from the one you love most. You must have the strength to say: *No. This is not acceptable. I will not serve this.*

You must love yourself so deeply that supporting your own suffering feels like a betrayal.

If you keep siding with your own misery, what else can ever come to you?

# 131 | The Plumcake or the Truth?

> *Fleeting sadness can be soothed by worldly comforts, but the deepest freedom comes from enduring pain that dismantles the ego.*"

As long as you live a socially adjusted but inwardly compromised life, even your sadness will remain shallow. You cry for a while, then someone hands you a plumcake, a gift, a distraction, and you feel alright again. The tears dry up, the discomfort fades: not because anything was resolved, but because the mind was pacified with a substitute.

Isn't that how sadness is usually handled?

*She's upset, buy her something.*

*He's down, take him out.*

Sometimes, you feel sad just because you want the gift, the attention, the comfort. Such sadness is just another form of demand. It isn't deep. It isn't transformative. It's just a tactic of the ego.

But when you truly want to break free—not just from sadness, but from the entire cycle of pleasure and pain, this pattern we call life—then your agony sharpens. It doesn't seek consolation. It seeks truth.

## The Plumcake or the Truth?

That kind of pain cuts through you. It doesn't just hurt the body or emotions, it pierces the ego. And in that cut lies real freedom. Not relief. Not comfort. But liberation.

Even such freedom comes with pain. The cut hurts. But it is clean. It is honest. Live through it. Don't give in. Don't reach for the plumcake. Don't settle for consolation.

Love is worth the wound, because the wound, when rightly received, becomes the doorway to something far beyond the self.

# 132 | Say Hello to Pain

> *Pain is unavoidable.*
> *But illusions aren't."*

There is pain from random changes over which you have no choice.

Be indifferent to such pain.

There is pain from the right kind of change you consciously choose.

Welcome that pain. Then there is pain from stupid actions and foolish decisions.

Why be stupid, and bear unnecessary pain?

Pain is unavoidable. Life keeps moving. But the body and mind crave stability. Pain arises when your urge to hold on collides with life's demand to keep shifting.

What is suffering?

Suffering begins the moment you believe life must be free of pain.

If you think you were born only for pleasure, you are bound to suffer.

Suffering is childish resistance to pain.

*Life should have been smooth. Where did this pain come from? I don't want it. I deserve happiness.*

That's how suffering starts: by refusing to accept pain.

So smile and say: *Hi, pain. Welcome, buddy. Care for a drink?*

And then: *Come right in. Don't hesitate. Strip me of illusions. Don't I look ready?*

# 133 | Pain in Installments

> *If you cannot take it on the chest, you cannot live by the heart.*"

We rarely confront the consequences of our actions head-on. And even when they do catch up, they don't strike as one clean, undeniable blow. You don't often see a single, deep wound across the chest.

Instead, the mind fragments the impact. One piercing truth is split into a hundred small, manageable cuts. The wound remains, but it is diluted, deferred, disguised, postponed.

Had suffering come all at once, intense and unmistakable, perhaps we'd have to stop, pay attention, and acknowledge reality. But we've designed our lives to prevent that. We split the impact, distort the pain, numb the discomfort. We trade clarity for convenience, truth for tolerability.

Even those small pricks don't come together. They arrive spaced out, with just enough time to recover, just enough relief to say: *I'm coping. This is normal.*

And so the illusion persists. We keep collecting minor wounds, never pausing to ask: What exactly am I protecting?

## Pain in Installments

To live by the heart is to be exposed. It means you take the hit directly, without filters or fragmentation.

If you cannot take it on the chest, you cannot live by the heart. The heart does not negotiate with dishonesty.

# 134 | You Repeat the Same Mistake a Hundred Times

> *As long as you remain the same, your mistakes will remain the same. Why even call them mistakes?"*

Has there ever really been such a thing as a new mistake? Look closely. That which unsettles you today is fundamentally the same thing that defeated you five years ago.

Names change. Faces change. Situations change. But has the underlying tendency changed at all?

The place of the fall changes. The hour of the fall changes. The excuse for the fall changes. But the fall itself, does it ever change?

You say: *This time it's different.* But is it? Or is it the same old pattern dressed in new clothes?

You are not making new mistakes. You are simply recycling old patterns in fresh disguises.

But man is cunning. He tumbles into the same pit twenty times, each time insisting the hole is new.

That is not a mistake anymore. That is a pattern. A refusal to learn. A commitment to unconsciousness.

## You Repeat the Same Mistake a Hundred Times

A mistake is something you make once. Twice becomes a habit. Thrice becomes a lifestyle. Beyond that, it becomes your very identity.

Stop calling them mistakes. Call them what they truly are: yourself.

# 135 | You Consent to Your Suffering

> *Choice! Choice! You are not helpless. Wake up to your power. You cannot just be carried away. Nothing can happen to you without your consent."*

When you are suffering, there is always a tendency to blame someone or something. We all want freedom from suffering. But can there be freedom without responsibility? Unless you fully accept the responsibility to end your suffering, there is no real liberation from it.

Understand this carefully. We are not talking about the person or event that triggered your pain. The point is simple: because you are the one suffering, you have the biggest stake in ending it. Blaming the culprit rarely helps, even if they are correctly identified.

Sometimes we say our suffering comes from random, uncontrollable events. And if suffering is merely incidental, how can there be freedom? External events are unpredictable. Pain often comes uninvited. But here is the difference: pain is external and situational, suffering is internal. You may not control pain, but suffering is often a matter of choice.

First, you must clearly see that suffering is not necessary. It is optional. You cannot suffer without your consent.

## You Consent to Your Suffering

Not just your consent, your participation is needed. In fact, suffering requires your active involvement.

That may sound absurd. Why would anyone choose to suffer? Because we have been conditioned to find some virtue in suffering. It attracts sympathy, self-righteousness, a sense of moral superiority, and sometimes even compensation, material or emotional. A crying face seems more deserving than a smiling one. We are taught, in countless subtle ways, to turn tears into virtue.

And when tears are seen as virtuous, there will obviously be more tears than smiles.

Suffering is not destiny. It is an unfortunate choice. Freedom begins when you understand this.

# 136 | Outgrow the One Who Erred

> *The harshest sentence you can deliver to yourself: I refuse to stay the same. Don't punish the mistake; outgrow the one who made it."*

Punishment must be productive. It must correct, not avenge. That alone is its purpose. Punishment cannot be an exercise in moral vanity.

Real punishment does not target just the action, the event, or the moment. It targets the doer, the tendency within you that keeps repeating the error.

And what is the punishment you deliver? Non-existence. When you see yourself producing unwanted results, you say to that old tendency: *You no longer deserve to exist. You must go.* This is what the ego hates most— change.

That is the only useful punishment: transformation. Refuse to remain the person who made the mistake. Refuse to empower the same tendency that keeps you stuck. *I am no longer the one who needs punishment,* that is the highest sentence you can impose upon yourself.

## Outgrow the One Who Erred

Do not remain who you are; otherwise, your mistakes will remain exactly as they are. Use your guilt wisely. When guilt is sincere, it becomes a catalyst. It triggers deep change.

Guilt that doesn't lead to real transformation is mere moral theatre. Punishment that only inflicts pain without awakening you is nothing but ignorant revenge.

# 137 | The Fire Inside, the Ashes Outside

> *When the forests burn,*
> *it is the fire, the smoke, and the raging*
> *apathy of man's mind made visible.*
> *Man's inner deadness is devouring*
> *the outer world, deadness that no amount*
> *of consumption can resurrect."*

Deforestation of the Earth and de-spiritualisation of man's mind are not two separate tragedies. The forests are burning because the self has collapsed. Both are being ravaged by the same inner fire: man's greed, his false identities, his endless hunger to consume.

In his hunger to feel whole, man has set the world on fire. He has razed forests, poisoned rivers, blackened skies. Still, he is not satisfied. He will never be. Even if the entire universe is reduced to dust, his craving will remain.

Because man is chasing peace down the wrong road. He looks for contentment in bodily pleasure and mental noise. But peace is not pleasure. Fulfilment does not come from stimulation. And no, this is not a moral sermon. These are naked, observable facts.

There is fire in man's mind, and there is fire in the forests. One is visible, the other is not. But both are the same.

The burning trees are his burning thoughts. The smoke above is the fog in his mind. The devastation outside is only the mirror of the devastation within.

Lack of spiritual clarity is killing man from the inside and the Earth from the outside. What we call environmental collapse is just man's inner wreck crashing into the world.

Unless man turns inward, unless he meets himself, questions himself, dissolves the lie he lives in, he will keep turning the planet into a graveyard.

And he will celebrate it. He will name it progress. He will worship it as development. He will sell it as success.

But it will be nothing more than a funeral procession. A burnt-out species limping through the ashes of a world it never understood. A mind destroying everything it touches, just to escape its own deadness.

# 138 | Better Bleed for Truth Than Shine for Lies

> *The worst defeat is not failure. The worst defeat is knowing a battle is worthy, and still walking away."*

Before you strive to excel, ask: *What must I excel in?* Before you chase speed, ask: *Which direction deserves my steps?*

Speed comes later, direction comes first. It is far better to crawl on the right path than to fly down the wrong one, toward your own destruction.

Making the right choice is more important than being perfect at the right choice. Pick the right battle, even if you fumble. Pick the right task, even if you're not yet good at it.

You will stumble. You will learn. And if the cause is true, you will rise. Courage is choosing what must be done, even if you're not good at it. Even if it breaks you.

The battle you avoid is the one you were born for. You don't fail by falling, you fail by fleeing. When you choose a worthy battle, being beaten is alright, opting out of the arena is not. Truth doesn't ask if you're ready, it asks if you're honest.

But society has corrupted your compass. The body tempts you toward convenience. They whisper: *Do what you're good at. Pick what suits your strengths. Choose what brings success.*

That's not wisdom. That's fear with a mask. That's cowardice pretending to be strategy.

Real decision-making begins with one question: *What must be done, regardless of my current ability?* That is the question of a conscious mind. Ability comes with time. And the ability to walk the right path comes only by walking it. Waiting for ability can be endless.

Choose not what flatters the ego, but what purifies it, even if it breaks you, even if you bleed. Better to bleed for truth than shine for lies, because false victories are slow suicides.

If your cause is false, even your brilliance is a betrayal. But if the cause is right, then your failure is progress.

# THE CALL TO INNER FREEDOM

# 139 | Too Smart to Be Wise

> *Smartness that is driven by fear and greed is just another name for foolishness."*

When it comes to nonsense, see how successful we are. We want to please ourselves, and we somehow always find a way.

Like a rat slipping into a house, we know where the hole is. And if there isn't one, we dig it ourselves. All our cleverness is reserved for our petty pursuits.

Are we truly dumb? Not at all. In chasing our worthless goals, we show immense energy and commitment, enough to shake the skies. But when it comes to what actually matters, suddenly we go blank. Our forgetfulness, our dullness, our laziness, they all appear only when the right thing calls.

What is right? That which emerges from deep attention, from quiet clarity, from dispassionate seeing. That which is born of realization—not sensation, not emotion, not excitement.

Even in our acts of idiocy, our intellect is at work. We aren't stupid, we're just destructively smart. Sharp, but inwardly blind. Too clever for our own good.

Perhaps what we need is not more smartness, but inner simplicity. Not the simplicity of looks or habits, but the simplicity that comes from seeing the mind's games without deception: clearly, honestly, directly.

# 140 | If Everything Goes, What Remains?

> *"What you think of yourself, is that really you?"*

The way we commonly use the word 'ego' is often misplaced. We confuse pride for ego. We mistake a particular kind of attitude for ego.

Someone struts around, puffed up, and we say he has an ego problem. But that's a very hazy usage.

Ego is simply 'I am'. Whatever you believe this 'I am' to be, that is ego.

'I am great' is ego. 'I am weak' is ego too. Whenever you say "I am" and follow it with an identity, a condition, a belief, that's ego in action.

We often think ego only means having grand ideas about oneself. But if someone believes they've been a lifelong victim, that too is ego. If someone says they are humble, modest or lowly, that's ego as well. Whatever I think of myself—good, bad, or ugly—is all ego.

I am none of what I imagine myself to be. All identities have been picked up. You didn't choose your family, gender, or religion. Yet over time, these get internalised and become what you call the 'self'.

In most cases, it's easy to see that what we call 'inner' has either been picked up randomly or handed over by someone else. And whatever comes from outside is not truly yours. If your sense of self is built on things you never chose, how can it be you?

Most things are accidental. You didn't choose your place of birth, your skin colour, or even your basic temperament. You haven't chosen to be thirty or forty as you read these lines. And if you're identified with any of this, you are identified with ego.

Now comes the real challenge. If you drop these accidental things, almost everything you've called your life disappears. And that creates fear: a deep, existential fear. Because when the things you thought were "you" vanish, it feels like *you* are vanishing.

If everything goes, what remains?

Only You.

What is that 'You'?

Intriguing, isn't it?

# 141 | Am I Fulfilled? Who Cares!

> *Real success is not about winning the world; it is about not being defeated by yourself."*

One is restless, one is restless, one is restless. Then one gathers the courage to look at the restlessness and finds nothing but pettiness there. That ends the need to keep attending to the restlessness.

Freed from the need to serve personal disquiet, one finds space to dedicate herself to something bigger. The bigger cause consumes so much attention, time, and energy that one is left with nothing to complain of, or even to wonder whether one is personally fulfilled.

One says: *Even if I remain personally unfulfilled, it is a small matter. I might be happy, I might be sad: it's fine. What I have submitted to is bigger than my little happiness and sadness. Does it matter how I'm feeling? Am I in pain? Oh, probably yes. But I just forgot that.*

This is beyondness. Or call it love.

*Have my troubles disappeared? No, they haven't.*

*Am I personally fulfilled? Probably not.*

*But who cares! I have something better to attend to.*

This is fulfillment.

## Am I Fulfilled? Who Cares!

When thoughts of your personal success stop mattering to you, when you say: *There is something more important than my personal success*, then you have really succeeded.

# 142 | Has Life Even Begun?

> *If one doesn't know what to live for, then life hasn't even begun."*

If you are burdened by the clock, enslaved by the hours, it is a damning indictment of your purpose.

Have the right reason for an action—a reason born not from external dictates, but from your deepest clarity—and you will instantly cease counting hours, whether it's for studies, for work, or for the very breath you take.

And as a young person especially, it is your fierce, unavoidable duty to forge these right reasons in life, to carve out a purpose that is genuinely yours. This is not a crowd phenomenon; it is intensely, excruciatingly personal. You cannot cower and whine: *Nobody else is doing such a thing, so why should I?* You have your own singular, fleeting life to live. Do not surrender it to the collective stupor.

Dare to figure out something truly worthy of your precious time. Then, and only then, will time rush to meet its rightful, potent utilization. And if something is finally being utilized rightly, why would you ever dare to limit that utilization? Then, any number of hours, any amount of effort, can be poured into it, for it will no longer be mere labor, but an expression of your deepest self.

Remember, time does not "fly away"; it rigidly follows your values. If it feels lost, it is because you value unconsciousness, you value external validation. Break free.

This is the ultimate act of self-love: to awaken to your power, to choose what truly matters, and to live with an inner completeness that fears no external outcome.

This is the only way your life truly begins.

# 143 | Better a Bloody Nose Than a Bleeding Heart

> *When you choose a worthy battle, being beaten is alright. Opting out of the arena is not alright. The worst defeat is when you know a battle is worthy, yet you shy away from fighting."*

First of all, your target must be worthy enough. Worthy targets are seldom easy. You don't choose them for comfort or convenience.

It might be speaking the truth in a fearful place, staying kind when bitterness tempts you, or pursuing inner clarity when the world is loud and messy.

None of this is easy.

In pursuance of a worthy target, small defeats are inevitable. Let them not mean too much. If you are too disturbed by small defeats, you won't stay put for long. You'll be so ashamed, so rattled, that you'll quit.

Take the small defeats in your stride. Brush them aside, so the bigger defeat stays at bay. What is the bigger defeat? To give up on a worthy purpose.

Let's be clear about what truly matters. The small defeats, you cannot avoid them. The big defeat. you can avoid it.

## Better a Bloody Nose Than a Bleeding Heart

Stay put. Take the blows right on the chin. It's better to have a bloody nose rather than a bleeding heart.

# 144 | The Body Will Veto Liberation

> *"Don't leave things as they are. Don't go with the flow. Time will not fix you. Experience will not awaken you. You could live forty thousand years, and nothing would change by itself."*

We are pleasure-seeking and effort-avoiding people. Look at a human being, or a creature of any species, we just do not want to work too hard. If you want to make a person work, you have to incentivise him. If you do not want to make him work, you don't have to do anything. Seeking the comfort of inertia is our default state.

Liberation is the highest of all achievements, and also the toughest of all destinations. Fighting one's bondages is the most important, but also the hardest task in life. Therefore, our biological tendency is to avoid liberation as much as possible, or at least delay it. Why? Because we don't want to work. We don't want to pay the price. We don't want to pass through the cleansing fire.

But you just cannot avoid the inevitable. Your comforts and conveniences won't last long. The security you assign yourself by remaining within your mental structures won't give you what you long for.

External securities that come from money and prestige won't help. And the internal security that comes from operating within one's zone of approval and disapproval, likes and dislikes won't help either.

So, freedom from bondages is what we all have to live for, consciously or unconsciously. The difference among people then lies in the path they take for their liberation.

This needs fundamental clarification. When you say you want to take a path of your choice, whose choice are you referring to? Who is the one making that choice? There are two of you: the one that must be liberated, and the one that delays liberation.

You are two, and these two are always at war with each other. At the same time, they coexist. You cannot make a decision without the other being involved. The body cannot decide on its own, and neither can consciousness take decisions unilaterally.

It is a strange situation. These two don't like each other, but are inseparable. It is a strange kind of wedding. They cannot be equal, because they belong to different dimensions. One has to be given precedence over the other.

If life is to be lived rightly, consciousness must be accorded greater value. The body must follow the guidance of consciousness. That is the only harmony possible between the two.

Between consciousness and the body, you cannot go for collective decision-making. If you give equal weight to both, then the body will keep vetoing liberation, and the real thing will never happen. Yes, the body must be heard, but it must never have the final say.

# 145 | Already Home

> *There are those who start for a destination, and then there are those who start from the destination. The latter are home even if they do not reach."*

Those who believe the world holds something truly worth attaining wander in hope.

Then there are those who play with the intensity of a champion athlete, yet remember it's just a game. They are free. They fight with full strength, but not from a place of existential insecurity.

The former may or may not reach. The latter never left: they are home, even on an unfinished path.

It is never the situation that defeats you. Situations are external. They come and go: temporary, unpredictable events.

Defeat, on the other hand, is internal. And everything internal is your territory, governed by your choice.

Adversity does not discriminate. Everyone faces setbacks, losses, reversals. Everyone watches plans collapse and momentum break.

What matters is how you respond. Do you shrink, retreat, resign? Or do you stand taller, even if bent, even if bloodied?

In moments of success, strength is easy. Victory creates many false heroes.

But the real test lies elsewhere. To remain dignified in defeat, to fight cleanly even when the cause seems lost, that is rare. That is noble. That is real.

Defeat can become your burial ground, or your battleground. Better still, let victory and defeat both be your playground.

Those who know what they stand for, those who start from the destination, keep walking regardless. They are already home.

Their steps are not reactions. They are declarations of inner security.

# 146 | Play through Pain

> *Play through pain.*
> *Play in pain. Just keep playing!*
> *Pain is life."*

If you're truly immersed in something worthwhile, do you really have the bandwidth to fuss over pain? Pain is there, yes, but it becomes peripheral. It doesn't dominate your attention. It doesn't hijack your purpose.

Even an average sportsperson knows this. When you're chasing something as basic as victory in a game, pain becomes secondary. Unless it's crippling, unless they're carrying you off on a stretcher, you keep playing.

The noon sun is blazing. The heat is unbearable. Do they stop to complain? Do they negotiate with the weather? No. The sun is where it must be. The body is where it must be. Why aren't you where you must be?

Why are you wandering? Why are you existentially homeless? Why are you still seeking comfort when the call is for commitment?

Pain never fully disappears. It's not a glitch; it's part of the design. Life keeps offering pain. That's the deal. But there's something deeper than pain, something that doesn't ask for relief, only direction.

When you're aligned with that deeper thing, pain doesn't vanish, but it loses its grip. It becomes background noise. You're no longer negotiating with discomfort. You're too busy living.

You must live from a place inside that pain can't touch. That impregnable place — that is your real home.

# 147 | Our Programmed Emotions

> *Emotions are not innate, they are expressions of conditioning. Just as thoughts arise from mental patterns, emotions arise from physical and social patterns."*

Even before you feel an emotion, its chemical buildup has already begun.

Emotion is mental activity, like thought, but deeper, more intense, and more unconscious. It arises from a more primitive layer of the mind and carries the weight of the body. That's why emotions feel overwhelming: they are saturated with hormonal and evolutionary energy.

GIven our lack of understanding, we take emotions to be something sacred, more authentic, more heartfelt than thought. That is a mistake. What we call emotion is often nothing more than a surge of animal inheritance. We share anger, fear, lust, and attachment with every wild creature in the jungle. The body is the source, and hormones are the triggers.

If the physical body provides the fuel for emotion, society gives it the direction. One person weeps at a funeral, another at a cricket match. The trigger varies, the structure remains the same.

The way to uncover your conditioning is through attention: watch your emotions as they arise. See their rhythm, their origin, their hold. As you observe them, their grip weakens. And when conditioning weakens, you don't become numb, you become sensitive.

Freedom from emotion is not deadness. It is freshness. You begin to notice things you had always ignored. The sunlight on your arm. A stranger's tone. A moment of silence. You become less emotional, but more alive.

Emotions are stale. You already know what will make you angry, what will make you cry, what will please you. It's all programmed. The same things provoke the same reactions again and again.

Sensitivity is different. Sensitivity means freshness. To be touched by life without filter, without prediction. Like splashing cold water on your face in the morning. Awake. Present. Clear.

# 148 | You Become What You Absorb

> *Be very particular about the company that you keep; nothing changes you better and faster than the right company."*

Of all the forces that shape life, none is stronger than the company and environment you allow yourself. So, be vigilant. Be watchful about the people you meet, the words you read, the food you eat, what you watch, and what you hear.

Do not let things enter you indiscriminately.

Yes, a point comes when you can drop all caution. A point comes when your inner clarity is so strong that you no longer need any outer defenses. But until that point arrives, be alert. Be very careful.

The senses are absorbing every moment. And you become whatever you absorb.

# 149 | How Much Darkness Did You Leave Behind?

> *Life's true measure is not in what you gain, but in how much of your inner darkness you leave behind each day"*

Ask yourself just one question:

Is the way I am living reducing my inner darkness?

This inquiry—simple, blunt, unwavering—tells you whether you're living rightly. There is no second question. This is the mirror. Everything else is noise.

It doesn't matter how well-fed you are, how finely tailored your clothes, how wealthy you've become, or how reputed and respectable you appear. These belong to the outer world, and they carry almost no weight in the realm that truly decides your life's direction: the inner one.

The real question is: Are you walking away from your darkness, moment by moment, day by day, choice by choice?

Are your actions thinning the fog inside?

Are your decisions slicing through confusion, or adding to it?

It is alarmingly easy to waste life. The decades pass like smoke, without ceremony, without warning. One moment you're in school, the next your joints ache. Time flies not because it is fast, but because you weren't paying attention.

Unless you bring great caution, through conscious clarity, life will almost inevitably slip through your fingers. Not because you wanted to waste it, but because you were programmed to.

That is the default script. You are born into a world designed to keep you busy, distracted, competitive, entertained—anything but liberated. You are not trained to face your darkness. You are trained to mask it.

It is a script cast in stone.

Well, almost.

Because stone, under the right pressure and heat, can crack. And once you start asking the real question, the script begins to fracture. It no longer holds the power it once had.

# 150 | This Is Not Your Destiny!

> *Your true self is not something you become; it is something you uncover. The true self is not to be searched for. The false self is the searcher."*

Never forget your essential reality, far beyond the reach of your immediate experiences. You are truly immense, powerful beyond measure, though nothing in the way you live, eat, breathe, or think seems to testify to it. Your habits don't reflect it. Your choices don't express it. But it remains true: untouched, undiminished.

We exist in a state of compulsive helplessness. Looking at our lives, it feels absurd to believe we are potentially free beings. But freedom is our essential nature. Which means we are never truly puppets. Even if you find yourself enslaved — by systems, relationships, emotions — that bondage exists only with your silent consent.

And unless you admit this, unless you take full ownership of your inner surrender, you cannot remember your true self. You will keep blaming, deflecting, rationalizing, and remain disconnected from your own power.

## This Is Not Your Destiny!

If you keep insisting that you are struggling, defeated, and forced, then your own belief will become your false destiny. You will live out the story you've written in fear. You will forget that you were always free, and that remembering is the first step to reclaiming.

# 151 | Remember the Truth, Not the Noise

> *Never forget who you are. Forget that, and you'll start living lies."*

Not everything you remember is worth remembering. Most of your past is noise, not wisdom. Drop it, and you'll find peace.

Not all that you know deserves to be known. Much of it is borrowed, irrelevant, dead weight. Let it go, and you'll feel lighter.

Not everything you have needs to be had. Let possessions serve you, not rule you. You'll remain humble.

And what you don't have, see that it's rarely essential. Lack is not a curse. Often, what's missing is what you don't truly need. You'll remain free.

True remembrance is not clinging to trivia, but staying rooted in Truth. When you remember rightly, you live rightly. And right living is silent liberation.

Constant remembrance is unending freedom.

# 152 | Stop Meditating, Go Watch TV

> *Meditation that doesn't change life is just a lullaby for the mind. True meditation permeates through life, altering all that you are and all that you touch."*

Meditation must seep into every corner of your being, dismantling all that you are and all that you pretend to be.

Real meditation is the raw courage to let your life be torn apart and reassembled. If you keep sitting with closed eyes but refuse to let anything shift, your meditation is nothing but polished hypocrisy.

And when I say life must change, I'm not referring to some vague inner glow. I mean the hard facts: your relationships, your work, your diet, your spending, your politics, your surroundings. That's what life is. That's what consciousness is made of, that's the very stuff of mind.

If your dealings with clients remain the same, if your relationship with your family is just as petty, if your greed, your consumption, your opinions remain intact, then what exactly have you been doing on the mat?

Meditation that leaves your life untouched is not meditation at all. It is just another way to remain comfortably asleep. If the very centre of your being is not shifting, then your meditation is not transformation. It's sedation.

Real meditation is fire: if nothing is reduced to ashes, you are only daydreaming. Better to watch TV honestly than to meditate dishonestly.

# 153 | Dig the Dirt, Find the Diamond

> *Your inner diamond lies buried beneath your own inner dirt. Dig the dirt, dig it deep."*

Wherever you are, that is exactly where the door will open. You don't need a new city, a new relationship, a new teacher. Begin where you stand.

If you are bored, boredom is the door. Face it, enter it. If you are attached, that attachment is the door. Let it show you your neediness, your illusions, your blindness.

If you are angry or afraid, then your anger and fear are the gateway. Don't suppress them, follow them inward. They reveal the very architecture of your false self.

Whatever you are, start there. Don't wait for an ideal mood or a quiet hour. Start where it hurts. Start where it's messy. Start where you actually are.

Dig without flinching. Don't polish the surface or sanitize the dirt. Go through it. Only by piercing the layers can the diamond be revealed.

The dirt is not your enemy. It is the map. It holds the clues, the conditioning, the very shape of your mind.

# 154 | Break Out of Your Shell

> *Love for the Sky expresses itself as disgust for the cage."*

At some point, the chick must realize that the shell of the egg is just too small to spend a life in. It was fine once: warm, protective, necessary. But now? It's a prison.

How does the shell crack? Not by external force. It cracks because the chick refuses to stay small.

But unlike the chick, you don't have just one shell. You break one, and there is another. And another. And another.

Each shell is a belief. Each shell is a comfort zone. Each shell is a lie you have made peace with.

So what must you do? Grow from within. Grow bigger. Grow so big that the shell cannot contain you. Let your bigness, your clarity, your longing, your resolve, become unbearable for the shell.

The shell will not crack because you hate it. It will crack because you have outgrown it.

If you remain a little chick, the shell will never yield. And the sky will remain a dream.

But if you truly love the sky, you will not tolerate the shell. You will not decorate it. You will not call it home.

You will break it.

# 155 | Ignore the Small

*Ignore the small battles. Fight the right one, and only the right one."*

*I* will beat him!

I will destroy her! She dared to insult me, did you hear that? Did she, or didn't she? Was that a dig? A provocation? Was I wronged?

Pause. Have some mercy on yourself. Spare yourself the agony of these minor wars. They take your energy, your hours, your mental bandwidth—and in return, they give you nothing that nourishes.

Learn to bypass the small issues. They will come. They will tempt you. They will appear urgent and personal. But in truth, they are distractions. Choose instead to ignore the trivial in favor of what truly matters. Choose clarity over reaction, purpose over ego.

And every time you do this, celebrate it. Pat yourself on the back. Say: *That's one little step forward.* One step away from noise. One step closer to truth.

Life will throw endless bait, but the real task is not to bite. The real task is to preserve yourself for the real battle. Let the petty go. Focus your attention, your life, on the worthy.

# 156 | The Cage Was Never Outside

> *Whatsoever exists within or around you at the cost of your freedom is a cage.*"

You are a bird. Your nature is to fly. You don't need to be taught how to fly, only freed from the cage.

But we are strange creatures. Instead of unlocking the door, we train the bird to flap its wings *inside* the cage. And we call that spiritual effort.

Who are we fooling with these flying lessons? The bird doesn't need instruction. It needs space. It needs the sky. You don't need to gain anything. You need to drop what is false. That dropping—*that riddance*—is freedom.

Unlock the door. Let the bird out. You'll see: the comforts of the cage and the fear of the sky were trivial all along. Flight is not a luxury. It is your birthright.

And the cage? It was never outside. The cage is within.

# 157 | Time Doesn't Fly, You Drift

> *Time doesn't fly, it follows your values. If it's slipping away, it's because you're not clear on what truly matters. Clarify what matters, and watch your time rush toward it."*

You are the one allocating every moment: to distractions, duties, desires. And you do so precisely in line with what you consider valuable, whether consciously or not.

Time is not a mystery. It is a mirror, reflecting your inner hierarchy of importance.

So if you say: *I don't know, time just flew away,* you're not being innocent. You're being dishonest.

Time doesn't flee. It moves exactly where your mind tells it to. And if you say: *It slipped away unconsciously,* then understand this: unconsciousness is what you valued in that moment. Just as clarity is a choice, so is unconsciousness, and a costly one.

When you are fiercely clear about what is essential, you'll witness time obeying that clarity. No more slippage. No more confusion.

Strive for clarity. Without it, life will bleed out through the cracks of your own indecision

# 158 | One Day Has Infinite Time

> *The one who knows that the clock is ticking will not let the moment return empty. To respect life is to respect time.*

One day holds infinite time. You call it twenty-four hours only because you have chosen to define an hour in a certain way.

A day has just twenty-four hours, but how many minutes does a day have? Look: time has already multiplied.

You want even more? Count the seconds in a day. Time expands further.

And even a second has a billion fractions, does it not? See how time has become inexhaustible.

This is not just wordplay. Let a second mean to you what an hour does. Has not your wealth of time multiplied instantly?

One day carries endless possibilities. Yet look how you devote this infinite treasure to all kinds of trivialities, and then complain you are short of time.

Be ruthlessly mindful of where your time is going. Every billionth part of a second is life itself, and you throw it away as if it were nothing.

## One Day Has Infinite Time

A second is not an inconsequential unit. For you, it is the totality of time itself. If you want to honour life, start by honouring the second.

# 159 | You're Not Lazy. You're Loveless.

> *The cure for laziness?*
> *A heart on fire or a life worth*
> *fearing to waste."*

Laziness is not a lack of energy. It's a lack of understanding. You don't know your own inner terrain. So you don't know what kind of work will bring you joy, what kind of action will yield real dividends.

Work demands energy. And if the returns on that energy are unclear, you'll choose inaction over action. That's what laziness is. Had you tasted the sweetness—the sheer ambrosia—of right action, you would pick it over sloth every single time. Because what's the thrill in lying unconscious on a bed? Being awake is incomparable: awake, alive, and fully aflame.

Two forces can pull you out of laziness: either the fear of wasting your one precious life, or the love of something so beautiful, so immense, that you can't sit still. And I am talking about the right kind of fear: *I have only this life, and it terrifies me to waste it in mediocrity.* That is a fear worth having. Or the right kind of love: a burning heart, a bleeding heart, mad for something higher.

The courageous mind doesn't solve the problem. It solves itself.

# 160 | Stop Waiting to Be Saved

> *Your primary responsibility is toward yourself. Bring light and freedom to yourself. Only then can you bring them to others."*

You neglected what you should have done for yourself, and now you expect someone else to compensate for it.

The fundamental responsibility to bring clarity and richness into your life is yours alone. No one else was born to do it for you. Yes, others can willingly and voluntarily contribute, but it's not an obligation you can impose on them, nor do you have any right to feel betrayed if they refuse to shoulder your expectations. The bare fact is: your life, your responsibility.

To drag someone into your life and hope they will decorate it with meaning and beauty, isn't that naive? If you refuse to sweep your own house clean, why must someone else pick up your broom?

Still, you expect. And when the fantasy collapses, you feel wronged and play the victim.

Why manufacture sorrow on purpose?

# 161 | You Are Not Born Alone

> *Treat the body as your neighbour, a useful neighbour you must work with. But never let the neighbour walk into your house and become the owner."*

You are born welded to the body. You and the body arrive together, yet it is tricky for the two of you to truly be together. The nature of consciousness and the nature of the body are fundamentally different. Consciousness longs for freedom; the body thrives in repeating its ancient patterns.

These two are forced to share the same address. Body without consciousness is a corpse. Consciousness without the body has no stage to perform. But sharing a roof does not mean equality.

One must rule: the higher one, the more intimate one, and justifiably so. It is your life, and you must rule. The body is to you; you are not to the body.

It is never a relationship of peers. Either you will rise in the authority of awareness, or you will kneel to the body's compulsions. You will have to show your sovereignty over this animal machinery. You must conquer the body, or be ruled by it.

Is this conquest a matter of violence? No. It is a matter of clear seeing: understanding the restless nature of the body and the luminous nature of consciousness.

This understanding itself is victory. This victory is freedom.

# 162 | The Cage Feeds, the Sky Frees

> *We bow to the cage because it feeds us crumbs, forgetting the sky that could have been our feast. Freedom terrifies us, because it demands we grow our own wings and dare the vultures."*

We chant freedom, we worship it, we romanticize it. But when it actually knocks, we bolt the door and hide behind our comforts.

Why? Because the cage gives us goodies. The cage feeds us. The cage protects us. The cage says: *Stay here, little bird. I'll take care of you.*

Freedom? Freedom says: *Now you're on your own. No more free meals. No more guarantees. The sky is yours, go fly!*

And yes, the sky has eagles. It has vultures. It has storms. So we say: *Yes, it's a cage, but the food's decent. And who wants the eagles anyway?*

We don't want freedom. We want comfort. We want safety. We want someone else to take responsibility for our lives. We agree with the cage. We disagree with freedom.

But here's the catch: you will never be at peace in the cage. Because freedom is not a luxury. It is your nature.

## The Cage Feeds, the Sky Frees

You must ask yourself: Am I really alright with this? Because until you agree with freedom, you will remain restless. You will remain incomplete. You will remain a bird with wings folded in fear.

And one day, you will have to fly. Not because someone forces you, but because you will no longer tolerate crawling.

# 163 | Give Wings, Not Chains

> *If you love someone, give them wings, give them light, give them self-knowledge, and let them fly on their own."*

Any relationship that brings fresh bondage into your life is not love. It is a trap. A cage wrapped in flowers and perfume.

Can we look at the essence of relationship with some honesty, some insight?

Ask yourself: Does this person bring you roses or books? Pleasure or perspective? Is that not a clear enough indicator of what the relationship is really founded upon?

The fundamental curse of consciousness is body-identification. The more you are stuck in the body, the lower the life you will live.

In the company of this person, do you feel more like a body? Do they see you as a body? Do you look at them as a body?

Run. That is not love. That is regression.

What do you talk about when you're together? Is it wisdom, literature, philosophy, science, the state of the world—or mostly breasts and hips?

And what do you do when you are together? Do you nourish each other's understanding? Do you remind each other of

## Give Wings, Not Chains

something higher? Or do you simply indulge in the lowest common denominator?

Pay close attention. These are not small things. They are powerful indicators. You cannot fail to see them, unless you are determined to remain blind.

A relationship can elevate your life. It can be a ladder to the sky. But more often, it becomes the very weight that drags precious lives into mediocrity and darkness.

If you truly love someone, do not cling. Do not possess. Do not reduce them to a body.

Give them wings. Give them light. And let them fly.

# 164 | The Ancient Battle Within

> *To live free, you must relate to the body with awareness. Without it, the body will enslave you to its ancient patterns."*

You are not born alone. You arrive welded to the body. The two of you come together, but you cannot walk the path together forever.

Consciousness and the body are fundamentally different. Consciousness longs for freedom. The body craves repetition. Consciousness wants to fly. The body wants to crawl back into the cave.

And yet, they must remain together. The body without consciousness is dead. Consciousness without the body has no vehicle.

But do not be fooled, this is not a partnership of equals. One must lead. One must surrender. There is no peaceful coexistence here. No utopian harmony. Either you will live as the body, or the body will bow to your consciousness.

You must assert your authority. You must display your might. Because if you don't conquer the body, the body will conquer you.

## The Ancient Battle Within

And when it does, you will live as its slave, a puppet of ancient instincts, repeating patterns you never chose.

Is this conquest about violence? No. It is about understanding. It is about seeing clearly.

See the nature of the body. See the nature of consciousness. See their conflict. And in that seeing, you are already victorious.

This understanding is the conquest. And this conquest is freedom.

# 165 | Jump before You're Ready

> *Strength is not a reserve.*
> *Strength is a response."*

Most of us languish in a strange, suffocating confidence in our own powerlessness, our weakness, even our worthlessness. We are unsure about many things, but eerily certain of this one: *I don't have it.* Or at best, *I have it only up to a point.* And we have facts, memories, logic: a mountain of evidence to justify this quiet, self-inflicted humiliation.

To such minds, I won't even say that strength lies dormant within. If it did, you'd at least faintly sense its pulse. Strength explodes into existence only when a worthy challenge is courageously accepted. Courage doesn't mean the absence of fear. It means the refusal to let fear override the essential.

Strength isn't stored like savings, waiting for the right time. It isn't accessed, rather it is ignited the moment you step into a worthy battle.

It's not about unlocking reserves. It's more like something utterly new, unexpected, unimaginable, rising from nowhere.

Dare the challenge. Not because it is winnable, but because it is worthy. That's when you glimpse what was always possible, though forever hidden from the intellect.

## Jump before You're Ready

You must dare to give from empty pockets. Only then do you see they were never truly empty. You must love without assurance, speak without applause, fight without strength. It is in that choice—not for reward, but for what is right—that the inner vault bursts open.

If you wait to feel strong before stepping in, you will rot outside the arena. Your sword will rust, the battle will pass. And you will die untested, oblivious of your own unbirthed possibility.

Had Arjuna hesitated, waiting for 'full clarity,' would the Gita ever have descended? Never! Krishna's empowering wisdom did not come to someone perfect or pristine. It came to a man broken, confused, trembling. But crucially: present. That was the only currency that mattered. He didn't possess all the answers, but he showed up honestly. That honesty was the spark. Strength *followed*.

That is the terrible, beautiful secret: Do what you know is right, even if your guts scream 'not ready.' Do not wait for power. Do not grovel for certainty. Jump! Give before you feel abundant. Fight before you feel prepared. It is that audacious, uncompromising decision that blasts open the inner lock. How? Through a surrendered, desperate leap into what is right, even if the image of the result feels utterly unknown, or even terrifying.

Your treasure is never absent. It is simply uncalled, unsummoned. It will not yield to clever strategies or well-secured maneuvers. It bursts forth only when you leap nakedly into the unknown, clutching nothing but faith in the sheer rightness of the act.

What you mistake as absence is merely unbeseeched presence. You were never poor. Never weak. Never empty. You are just ignorant of who you are, and that knowledge comes only to those who have the faith to dare the unknown.

What unlocks the resources? Your decision to fight the battle, your decision to give even without having, your decision to leap blindfolded into the abyss.

# Jump before You're Ready

That trembling step into the arena—not with confidence, but with honesty— is everything.

# TRUTH: THE ONLY AUTHORITY

# 166 | The Past Stays Only If You Feed It

> *You don't forget the past by fighting it, you forget it by living fully in what truly matters now."*

Trying to forget the past is a sure-shot way of holding on to the past.

Do you know the two usual ways to remember something?

First—trying to remember it. Put up reminders here and there, and you will probably remember.

Second—by saying daily: *I want to forget it.* This is another way to remember something and never forget it. *I want to forget A, and so I remember daily to forget A.* And what am I remembering daily? A.

The mind knows well how to forget. Do you remember everything you have done since the morning today? No, you have already forgotten. The mind will forget on its own. But we forcefully do not allow the mind to forget.

How do we not allow the mind to forget a thing? By giving importance to that thing. The moment you take something seriously, it gets more deeply registered in the mind. So don't ask: *How to forget?* Ask: *How not to take trivia seriously?*

Our problem is that we take trivia seriously, and we have no sense of that which is really important. So we remember all the rubbish.

## The Past Stays Only If You Feed It

Sadly, in this obsession with trivia, that which is really important is forgotten. If you are absorbed in something very important right now, would the past come and bother you? If you are immersed in something immense, do random memories still come to haunt?

When does the past come to attack? When you are not present with the important.

Find out what is important. And stay with it, stick to it. Every moment one must ask: What is important? And the answer, irrespective of how it feels, must be honoured. Don't allow yourself to get drunken and drowsy.

Whenever you find that you are being carried away by a thing, ask:

*I ask in all my honesty and all my discretion, Is this thing important?*

If it is not important, it will drop on its own.

Someone asked: But how to know whether something is important? To know the answer, ask one more question: To whom is the importance or unimportance of a thing? All things hold importance, or the lack of it, to me. Hence, I am the touchstone. I am the criterion. Now what is important to me? That will be decided by my current state. My current state is of bondage, illusion, and indiscretion. So, that which brings clarity and freedom to me, that alone is important.

All else is trivia.

# 167 | A Heap of Unkept Promises

> *The mind seeks peace through everything it clings to. We latch onto anything promising completion, but true peace comes when we clear away all that which fails to deliver.*

Whatever enters the mind enters with a promise. The promise is: I will give you peace. If the entering object does not make this promise, it will not find a place in the mind. The promise is the non-negotiable condition for entry.

So, whatsoever exists in the mind does so on the back of the peace it promises.

The self feels inadequate and incomplete. If an object promises completion, the self attaches to it. It could be a thought, a vision, a person, an identity, or a hope. Whatever it is, is it giving what one really wants? Or is it more a source of inner strife? A needless and useless occupant of mindspace, that just squats within, and offers clutter in return?

Something is present in the mind. What is that presence doing to your life? What value does the presence add? How is your state when you are with that particular thought, or thing, or person? Do you feel at peace, or do you rather feel insecure? Does that object add to your confusion, or bring clarity to you?

## A Heap of Unkept Promises

If it is not giving you what you really long for, it is deadweight. Worse still, it could be a pathogen. Why let it remain?

Clear it away. That is clarity.

# 168 | The World Shakes Only the Shaken

> *The lover of Truth stands firm in Truth. Others oscillate between belief and doubt."*

Consider yourself shakeable, and everything will shake you. The smallest remark, the slightest change, the most trivial event: each will disturb your centre.

Consider yourself unshakeable, and see how things change. The same world, the same people, the same situations: now powerless to rattle you.

Consider yourself little, and everything will seem big enough to tease you. Every face intimidating, every challenge overwhelming.

Consider yourself immense, and see if the world can still bully you. Its tricks, taunts, threats: none will find a place to land.

But this consideration must run deep. It cannot be a tactic for tough times, nor a mask worn during crisis. To consider yourself immense is to live immensely, which means discarding pettiness, not occasionally or selectively, but as your very nature.

You must have something non-negotiable. Something untouched by opinion, fear, or temptation. A centre that is sacred and inviolable. Without that, you remain at the mercy of the winds. And winds have no mercy. They blow as they please. And you, without anchor, are blown with them.

# 169 | No New Path, Just New Eyes

> *Spirituality is not an escape from daily life, but the gentle light that helps you navigate daily choices with wisdom and clarity."*

If life is a journey, we are all walking. And most of us are walking in the dark, and blindfolded. The world taught us how to walk, but not where to walk, and certainly not why. Forget identifying the right path, the irony is, we don't even know who the traveller is.

Wisdom is not another road someone charts out for you. It is the power to see your current road, fully. It does not demand that you abandon your present life or take refuge in exotic philosophies. It invites you to look harder, deeper: to see the mud, the sunlight, the companions, and the curve ahead, with eyes unclouded.

Spirituality does not hand you divine GPS coordinates. It hands you a lamp, and says: Walk as you are, but walk lit.

You don't follow wisdom. You illuminate with it. You bring light to the terrain you already inhabit. And slowly, softly, you start to see where you've been, what beckons you forward, and most importantly, who is walking.

If change is necessary, it will arrive as a friend, not a force. And if truth must awaken, it will rise from within, not descend from above.

# No New Path, Just New Eyes

The sacred path is not separate from your daily steps. It is your steps, seen in light.

# 170 | The End of Motivation, the Start of Clarity

> *If motivation comes from outside, it will vanish when that outside force fades. No external spark can burn forever."*

When we chase a goal, we often believe: *Once I get X, I'll be complete.* Isn't that the familiar feeling?

*I'll be whole once I achieve this.* So, many ambitions are powered not by fullness, but by a quiet sense of lack.

*I'm not enough now, but once I reach that milestone, I'll deserve to feel better.* Our inner insufficiency becomes the engine of our striving. The deeper the wound, the faster we run toward a cure.

For many, fear becomes the fuel. The boss threatens, and work begins. But is that the only way to move? Must we always be pushed by fear or pulled by greed?

Don't ask for motivation. Don't wait to be threatened. That's the mindset of a mercenary: *Pay me and I'll act,* or worse, *Force me and I'll obey.* Is that the life you want? An endless cycle of carrot and stick?

Find your true engine instead: a force deeper than fear, greater than greed. With it, effort vanishes. Work becomes play. Movement becomes ease. The day no longer drags, you become the day.

## The End of Motivation, the Start of Clarity

When fear or greed rule you, where is the space for joy? At day's end, how many faces truly glow?

True action doesn't rise from motivation. It blooms from clarity.

Let work become a celebration. Let it be life itself. Wake not in dread but in quiet eagerness. Reach for your work as naturally as your breath, as steadily as your heartbeat.

Then work ceases to be toil, it becomes sacred expression. Not a burden, but your living truth.

# 171 | Don't Fear the Cost of Freedom

> *Freedom is possible if you drop your imaginations about the consequences of freedom."*

Freedom is possible. Life need not remain a sad, monotonous song. It can become a symphony of ecstasy. You must have that faith.

Don't surrender so easily to voices of littleness. They will whisper: *Who are you to want freedom? You're just a petty creature.* Don't listen. Simply because you are conscious, you have the right to be free.

Freedom is often blocked by fearful estimates of what it might cost. But most of what you fear is just mental projection, stories told to you or invented by yourself. Freedom feels dangerous only because the mind clings to old certainties, even when they hurt.

No matter your past, your present circumstances, or the actions you've accumulated, you are destined for liberation. As long as you are conscious, you have the right to be joyfully conscious.

And by Joy, I don't mean ordinary happiness or pleasure. I mean a deep fulfillment so complete that happiness and sadness become mere ripples on its vast surface.

Any price you pay for freedom appears big only while you remain unfree.

# 172 | Your First Love Must Be Your Highest Self

> *Your primary love affair must be with your own highest possibility. That's the first love worth having: a raging, relentless romance with your own greatness.*

The quality of your love depends on the quality of your life. If your life is soaked in mediocrity, your love cannot be sublime. We crave fairytale romances while living as frightened, greedy, petty creatures. But how can anything divine emerge from a swamp?

You want a love that is pure and powerful? First ask: What is the texture of your own being? Is it deep, clean, clear: or cluttered with neediness and confusion? Who will be drawn to a small, anxious self? What kind of love can such a self give or receive?

Live small, and you will attract smallness. In romance, in work, in friendships, in vision. Then comes the inevitable: heartbreak, bitterness, repetition. The same drama, the same disappointment, again and again. Because the source hasn't changed.

Why remain trapped in this tragic loop? Why blame the outside when the inside remains untouched?

## Your First Love Must Be Your Highest Self

Rise. Burn. Transform. Then see who enters your life. Then see what kind of love surrounds you. Not romance. Not pleasure. But the resonance of clarity and freedom.

# 173 | This Chemical Existence

> *Your thoughts and emotions are just biochemical things. They are obliged to follow their chemical agenda, even if it means your suffering.*

A single word strikes your ear, and there is instant upheaval. Your whole body heats up. One word, and your temperature shoots up by two degrees in minutes. What is this if not a chemical reaction?

This body is a heap of chemicals. Let the body be.

Let the chemical thoughts be. Let the chemical feelings be. Let the chemical emotions and sentimentality be. Let the chemical sexuality be. Let the chemical fears be. Let the chemical hopes and ambitions be. Let the chemical love be. Let the chemical death be. Let the chemical life be.

I am free. All this is just chemistry. What is chemical is a slave to its material composition. Why must I become its slave? Why must I be entangled in it?

# 174 | Relaxed. And Dangerous.

> *A relaxed man is a dangerous man. He has no doubts, so he cannot be manipulated. He has nothing to achieve, so he cannot be enslaved."*

Real relaxation is not about lying limp in a hammock or curling up in bed with your favourite lullaby. Real relaxation means relaxing even as the storms rage around you. You are relaxed as you sweat, as you run, as you bleed. You are relaxed even when you are wringing yourself dry. You are not a beggar waiting for some special 'relaxing' activity to be mercifully granted, like a weekend retreat or a fleeting moment in your child's laughter. You are simply relaxed, effortlessly, unconditionally, irrevocably.

You sit anchored in your inner stillness, and from there, you may choose to summon storms. You may pick up battles, burdens, and chaos—not because you must, but because you are free to.

You may look tense on the outside, but that tension has a different fragrance. It is never for your own petty security. It never penetrates your core. It is like waves thrashing on the surface of an unmoved ocean, or rain battering the flanks of an immovable mountain.

The relaxed man is not passive. He is not lazy. He is not indifferent. He is simply untouchable.

Relaxed. And Dangerous.

And that makes him very dangerous, to those who feed on others' bondages

# 175 | Succeeding, or Being Owned?

> *"What you take today from the world for your pleasure will tomorrow become a chain around your neck. You will find the world holding the other end of that chain."*

You think you're winning, but you're being conquered.

What we usually celebrate as worldly success is, in fact, the world's ruthless success over us. It is not you triumphing over the world, it is the world seizing you, owning you, bending you to its will. The world doesn't merely tempt you. It tames you. And then it brands that taming as your achievement.

The world is all over you. It screams in your choices, it breathes through your desires, it hides behind your ambition. And you call that *your* success?

No. It is the world's victory.

So, what is real worldly success?

It is to never allow the world to become too much for your mind.

It is to never allow the world's voice to drown your own.

It is to never let the world's wounds reach your centre.

## Succeeding, or Being Owned?

It is to never hand over your freedom for fame, money, approval, or comfort.

Real success is to not do what the world wants from you. It is to do what sets the world free from itself.

Worldly success is not about playing the usual worldly game better. It is about refusing to be a pawn in the first place. The true winner is not the one who masters the rules of the world, but the one who outgrows the game entirely.

So ask yourself, not: *How do I succeed in the world?* Ask instead: *How do I stop being ruled by it?*

Because until you break free from its grip, every reward it offers is just a stronger chain.

# 176 | Already Rich, Just Forgot

> *Before you accumulate something from outside, first figure out what you already have."*

We have been trained to believe wealth is something you must chase. Something you gather, display, cling to. Money, property, degrees, relationships, reputation, experience—all borrowed from the world.

But whatever the world gives, the world can take away.

Somebody gave you that reputation; somebody else can snatch it. Your image exists only in others' minds, and minds change overnight. You depend on what you have gathered. You start to think you are it. And now you live in fear, afraid of losing what never really belonged to you.

This is the hidden curse of accumulated wealth: it breeds insecurity. It ties you to endless anxiety.

But there is another wealth. A kind the world cannot touch. A wealth that does not arrive from outside but quietly shines from within.

Not what you have. What you are.

It is the light of your being. The silent radiance that remains when everything else is stripped away.

## Already Rich, Just Forgot

It is not about how bright your possessions look. It is about being the light that illumines all possessions.

Ironically, in your frantic race to acquire, you forget you are already rich. You forget the greatest treasure is already yours, safe and unstealable.

This wealth does not sit in your bank account. It lives in your being.

Find it before you go out seeking more.

# 177 | Find Your Flower

> *Real love tests. Real love stretches. Real love breaks. It is the sculptor's chisel hammering away at the unshaped rock, relentlessly and mercilessly, until beauty is unveiled."*

That which would bring you total satisfaction will never allow you to remain the petty creature you are. Vastness comes only to the vast. You are what you want. If you truly wish to change who you are, you must dare to want something utterly beyond your current self.

Your destination shapes your constitution. You become what you long to achieve.

If you love the mud, you will become an earthworm. If you love the Sky, you will grow wings. If you keep worshipping trivialities, you will remain trivial. But if you bow to something tremendous, your entire personality will be torn apart and rebuilt in its image.

To want something different, to take something dazzling and alien as your goal, you must go against yourself. You will have to endure the agony of transformation. Your whole system will be forced to break, to burn, to be reborn.

## Find Your Flower

They say, *It was the love of the flower that turned the caterpillar into the butterfly.* Without that impossible love affair, the metamorphosis could never happen.

So go. Find your flower. And surrender to it without compromise.

# 178 | Why Remain Small?

> *"You must learn to admire greatness. You must learn to submit and commit to what is valuable. Only then does it become possible to say 'no' to all the nonsense."*

We are not at fault for being born small: ignorant, insecure and reactive. That's how life begins for everyone. But we are absolutely responsible for *remaining* small.

The great one isn't born great. He's just the one who finally says: *Enough of this smallness.* He refuses to stay stuck. He chooses responsibility over comfort, clarity over confusion, and depth over distraction.

And that's what confronts us. If someone else could rise from our exact condition, why can't we? If greatness is possible, and it clearly is, then smallness is no longer innocent. It is a decision.

We often shield our mediocrity by mocking those who rise. We look for flaws in the high, not because they are flawed, but because we fear climbing ourselves. We take pride in our mediocrity and call it humility. But that's not humility, that's surrender to weakness.

## Why Remain Small?

We can't stay small and pretend to be virtuous. Growth begins when we *revere* what is truly worthy. We stay small because we never bow to the Great.

We want freedom without discipline, love without transformation, respect without earning it. But real change begins with submission: to Truth, and to what liberates us from falseness.

If we haven't submitted to anything higher, we remain ruled by everything lower.

Our problem isn't that we're small. It is that we refuse to rise.

# 179 | Choose a Goal You Can Never Reach

> *Work for the sake of greatness, and greatness is what you will get. Work for pettiness, and nonsense is what will follow."*

You must have a purpose so high it can never be fully attained. Because it cannot be completed, you will keep working toward it all your life, never slipping into the illusion that you have arrived. That endless humility is essential to endless diligence, and to a progressive movement into the endless.

And what is that final purpose? It is called realization. Liberation. The dissolution of the ego. Not achievement, not success, not recognition, but freedom from the one who craves all of that.

The ego cannot be dissolved by direct assault. It resists confrontation. It thrives on opposition. It softens only through the right lifework: through sustained, meaningful action that doesn't feed it.

You must therefore choose work that keeps sublimating the ego. Work that doesn't inflate your image, but quietly refines your being. Work that doesn't make you feel superior, but keeps you grounded and alert.

## Choose a Goal You Can Never Reach

And because the ego can never be fully and irreversibly liberated, you must keep the fire alive till your last breath. That is the method. No final victory. No retirement. No arrival.

Choose a goal so vast that you are always alert, always humbled, never complacent enough to say, *I am done. I can now retire.*

The path itself becomes the destination. And the movement itself becomes the liberation.

# 180 | Only Your Choice Matters

> *All powerlessness is just a pretense. Even in your feeblest moment, you are still powerful enough to exercise choice, and you must always hold this very close to your heart.*

No situation is ever so dark, so doomed, that you could excuse yourself from making the right choice. And no situation is ever so perfect, so luminous, that right choice becomes unnecessary. In joy or grief, in clarity or confusion, in sunshine or storm: anything can happen, at any time. The world does what it does. But you? You must decide.

Your response to situations is always a matter of your choice. Life isn't what happens to you. Life is how you respond to what happens to you. And your response is what truly happens to you. All else is fleeting images on an external screen.

Far from being weak, you hold a terrifying power. You are dangerously, gloriously free. You can choose what is right even in the worst of times. And you can choose what is wrong even when surrounded by every possible advantage. That is both the grandeur and the horror of being human.

This also means: the situation is never to be blamed. Your upbringing, your trauma, your distractions, your temptations: none of these can rob you of the power to choose rightly. At most, they influence. They never compel. You may be flooded with excuses, but never stripped of responsibility.

And that's the essential task: to awaken to your responsibility, not as a burden, but as your birthright. The power to choose is what makes you human. It is also what makes you divine.

Scream this truth to yourself if you must. Whisper it if you're afraid. Etch it into your being if you care to live rightly:

Situations do not matter. My choice, and my choice alone, matters.

# ABOUT THE AUTHOR

We live in a time when lies are sold with charm, and vagueness passed off as wisdom and entertainment as spirituality. Though materially empowered, we are inwardly more fractured than ever. Popular culture offers optimism, success, and fulfilment, yet quietly leaves behind fatigue and confusion. The deeper questions—'Who am I? What do I really want? Why does suffering persist?'—remain buried under noise, opinion, and false comfort. The result: personal, social, and global crises of a scale never before seen.

Acharya Prashant speaks directly to this condition. He doesn't decorate the disease; he diagnoses and exposes it. His teachings hold up a mirror to the mind. Relentlessly rational, deeply compassionate, and sharply original, he brings fierce clarity to modern life—not as theory or mystical escape, but as a radical dismantling of the false structures we live by.

For over a decade, he has engaged with real-life questions on love, fear, ambition, suffering, and ego through thousands of talks, books, interviews, and retreats. His style is unsentimental and piercing, yet full of quiet compassion. He does not trade in hope, but offers insight. He does not promote belief, but calls for intelligence.

Through the PrashantAdvait Foundation, he has revived interest in over seventy classic Indic spiritual texts, including the Upanishads, the Bhagavad Gita, and the Ashtavakra Gita. His books, courses, and public engagements attract seekers across all age groups, professions, and walks of life. His digital presence now forms the world's largest repository of wisdom literature. Today, he is the most followed wisdom teacher in the world, with an influence growing across generations and geographies.

Recognized for his impact, he has been honoured by the IIT Delhi Alumni Association for Outstanding Contribution to National Development, by PETA as the Most Influential Vegan, and by the Green Society of India as the Most Impactful Environmentalist.

His path has not been easy. He has spoken without fear, and the world has often responded with silence, hostility, or distortion. Rooted in clarity rather than comfort, his teachings have unsettled both religious traditionalists and modern conformists. The media ignored him. Institutions withheld recognition. Platforms censored him. Ritualists accused him of blasphemy. Academics dismissed him. He has been misquoted, attacked, shadowbanned, and deliberately excluded from spaces that claim to welcome wisdom.

He stood alone, without lineage, endorsement, or shelter from the storm. He refused to soften his words for approval. He never aligned with power, courted no popularity, played to no gallery. For years, he spoke in silence, to silence—not because he couldn't have drawn an audience, but because the Truth could not be diluted. That he is heard today is the outcome of tireless labour, an unshakable inner fire, and a message the world could not ignore. If his voice now reaches millions, it is not because the system supported it—but because the system could not stop it.

Unaffiliated with any lineage or sect, he speaks from direct realization, not inherited belief. This radical independence makes his voice both fiercely original and spiritually honest, free from the weight of tradition and the need for conformity.

In an age of noise and spectacle, he has chosen the hard path of clarity. That is why he is not easily celebrated: he neither flatters tradition nor panders to trends. But his teachings—scripturally grounded yet free of dogma, rational yet spiritually fierce—mark a turning point in the history of wisdom. In him meet the honesty of Buddha, the depth of Vedanta, and the immediacy of the digital world—without compromise.

As the noise of the present fades, his words will remain. Long after contemporary names are forgotten, his voice will shape how the sincere self approaches truth. His legacy won't be counted in fame, but in the transformations he ignites across generations. If the 21st century is remembered for one voice of truth, it will be his.

# A BRIEF BIOGRAPHY

**Early Life & Education**

Prashant Tripathi was born on the Maha Shivratri of 1978 in Agra, India. As a child, he stood out for his depth of attention and appetite for knowledge. He topped the ICSE board exams and was an NTSE scholar, yet his real education began beyond the classroom—through unrestrained reading, self-inquiry, and silent observation. With support from his father, a well-read bureaucrat, he explored books of every kind, laying the groundwork for a mind that would question everything.

In school and college, he emerged as a champion speaker, actor, and poet—respected for his command of both Hindi and English. He won national debates, directed acclaimed plays, and led intellectually vibrant cultural forums. Yet, even in the midst of success, he felt deeply out of place. The celebration of intellect without depth, ambition without meaning, left him restless. He felt inwardly estranged in institutions others idolized.

He graduated from IIT Delhi and later from IIM Ahmedabad, holding the rare distinction of clearing both CAT and UPSC in the same year. Even so, the world of conventional careers never held his interest for long. During his three-year corporate stint, he began using his weekends to teach leadership through wisdom literature. This initiative became the seed of a much larger movement.

## Advait Life: Education & HIDP

He soon founded Advait Life-Education, a pioneering initiative focused on self-awareness in education. Its flagship program—the Holistic Individual Development Program (HIDP)—reached over 50,000 students across more than 50 institutions. Personally designed and led by him, HIDP became a structured yet dynamic experiment in bringing spiritual insight into mainstream education. Its early success revealed what becomes possible when young minds are met with honesty, depth, and challenge.

## The Turn Within

In 2008, at age 30, he began decisively stepping away from institutional obligations to devote himself fully to the fundamental questions of human suffering and self-ignorance. What began as campus dialogues soon expanded into immersive sessions, retreats, and seminars. In 2011, he started conducting self-awareness camps in the Himalayas—intimate gatherings that continue to draw seekers from India and abroad. Based on rigorous scriptural study and inner work, these camps marked the beginning of his direct engagement with serious spiritual aspirants.

His departure from the world was not merely professional; it was existential. Renouncing ambition, comfort, and recognition, he chose inner discipline and silence. It is from this ground that his teachings arise.

## Global Reach & Digital Impact

Following his revival of over 70 classical spiritual texts through the PrashantAdvait Foundation, Acharya Prashant has continued to engage deeply with texts across time and tradition. He draws freely from diverse sources—from the Sermon on the Mount and the Tao Te Ching to Buddhist sutras, Sufi poetry, Zen koans, and the verses of Kabir Saheb, whom he reveres as one of the clearest and highest spiritual voices in history.

He often speaks on the writings of Nietzsche, Sartre, Camus, and Kierkegaard—not to agree or oppose, but as a spiritual examiner of existential anguish. His fondness for absurdist theatre—Beckett and Ionesco—as well as Kafka reflects his insight into the mind's desperate search for meaning. Yet, unlike despairing philosophers, he uses these voices to deepen—not dissolve—the movement toward liberation.

As a poet himself, his language carries clarity wrapped in rhythm, austerity steeped in grace. His teachings now form the world's largest digital archive of living wisdom, with over 30,000 freely available videos and articles, viewed more than 4.8 billion times.

He has authored over 160 books in Hindi and English, covering topics from self-awareness to society, scripture to science. He engages with seekers nearly every day, and his social media presence—now over 80 million followers—makes him the most followed wisdom teacher in the world. His Bhagavad Gita learning program has crossed 1,00,000 students, and in June 2024, he conducted the world's largest Gita exam.

## Broader Initiatives

Beyond personal growth, Acharya Prashant has brought rare clarity and courage to urgent global concerns—climate change, animal rights, women's empowerment, and the eradication of superstition. For him, social reform is a necessary outcome of inner individual clarity.

In a world that spiritualizes consumption and ritualizes cruelty, he has spoken with unmatched precision. He has exposed the hollowness of token environmentalism, arguing that the real climate crisis is one of human greed and ego. In 2025, he launched *Operation 2030*—a monumental campaign to confront the climate crisis not as a technical or political issue, but as a call to inner clarity, advocating deep change in how individuals live, how institutions function, and how society defines progress. He has relentlessly challenged meat consumption and religious animal slaughter, calling them acts of unconsciousness disguised as culture. His voice for animal liberation has reached millions, making him one of the most influential vegan figures globally.

On the question of women, he has called out the patriarchal mind—whether in domestic obedience, religious roles, or the myth of the 'divine feminine' used to keep women docile. His message: liberation begins not with imitation or defiance, but with awakening intelligence.

He has also launched campaigns against superstition, fake gurus, and blind faith—urging people to question, think, and walk free of inherited beliefs. His sessions and videos continue to shake cultural assumptions, reaching those seeking not political slogans, but true freedom.

All this, while continuing to meet thousands through public events, in-depth interviews, and rigorous online dialogues—each space an invitation to see through illusion and step into clarity.

## In Essence

Acharya Prashant's life stands as a rare embodiment of relentless clarity and total dedication to Truth. For those seeking not comfort but real change, his presence offers not just answers, but a radical shift in how life is seen and lived.

# HarperCollins *Publishers* India

At HarperCollins India, we believe in telling the best stories and finding the widest readership for our books in every format possible. We started publishing in 1992; a great deal has changed since then, but what has remained constant is the passion with which our authors write their books, the love with which readers receive them, and the sheer joy and excitement that we as publishers feel in being a part of the publishing process.

Over the years, we've had the pleasure of publishing some of the finest writing from the subcontinent and around the world, including several award-winning titles and some of the biggest bestsellers in India's publishing history. But nothing has meant more to us than the fact that millions of people have read the books we published, and that somewhere, a book of ours might have made a difference.

As we look to the future, we go back to that one word—a word which has been a driving force for us all these years.

Read.